Praise for Gwen ~~Cooper's Books~~

Praise for *Homer's Odyssey*

"Touching...one not to miss."

—*USA Today*

"This memoir about adopting a special-needs kitten teaches that sometimes in life, you have to take a blind leap."

—*People*

"Cooper is a genial writer with a gift for conveying the inner essence of an animal."

—*The Christian Science Monitor*

"Delightful...This lovely human-feline memoir, following in the footsteps of Vicki Myron's bestselling *Dewey: The Small-Town Library Cat Who Touched the World*, is sure to warm the hearts of all pet lovers."

—*Library Journal*

"Well written with...tenderness and realism...Your life will be richer for having taken this journey with [Gwen and Homer]."

—*I Love Cats* magazine

Praise for *My Life in a Cat House*

"This book perfectly encapsulates the unique and amazing experience of being owned by cats and the joy they bring into our lives. That alone is reason enough to read it."
—James Bowen, international bestselling author of *A Street Cat Named Bob*

"Cooper, who charmed readers with the best-selling memoir of her intrepid blind cat, *Homer's Odyssey*, returns with escapades of other past and present felines. Cooper's witty, breezy writing, her unabashed love of felines, and her admission that her spoiled cats have trained her will delight and resonate with cat people."
—*Library Journal*

"Fans of *Homer's Odyssey* will rejoice upon hearing that Homer's owner, Cooper, has returned with more true cat stories...both hilarious and deeply moving. Readers...will delight in these anecdotes of cats who seemingly have something to say about everything. Fans of Vicky Myron and Brett Witter's *Dewey* and James Bowen's *A Street Cat Named Bob* will be highly satisfied."
—*Booklist*

"If you've ever lived with a cat, then this book is for you ... In *My Life in a Cat House,* Cooper lovingly and humorously depicts the ups and downs of a life with cats and the ways in which they mimic human behavior and feelings. A fun read for all animal lovers."
—*New York Journal of Books*

"A literary fur fix for Homer fans!"

—Catster **magazine**

"As Gwen shares the joys, sorrows, laughter and tears of sharing her life with her cats, both past and present, you will find yourself nodding in recognition and perhaps remember the antics of a cat long gone. You may even gain a deeper understanding of your own feline companions."

—The Conscious Cat

"Gwen has the uncanny ability to touch our hearts with her gift of conveying thought-provoking and heart-stirring emotions...Gwen's writing is unpretentious, it's authentic, it's REAL. Whether like me you have nearly all of Gwen's books, or if this one is your first, you will delight in her descriptive, often hilarious and loving stories about her cats."

—Cat Chat with Caren and Cody

"There's something about Gwen Cooper's cat books that touch my heart like few others, and *My Life in a Cat House* is no exception. Whether you've enjoyed every one of Gwen's cat books or this is your first, snuggle up with a cat or two while you're reading. I guarantee with each turn of the page you'll pull them just a little bit closer as you realize just how empty your life would be without their unconditional love."

—Melissa's Mochas, Mysteries and Meows

"Gwen Cooper is the Queen of Cat Love—and in these fun and frisky stories, she perfectly captures all the reasons felines rule our hearts and our homes. No cat lover should be without this book, but more important, give it to the folks who haven't yet seen the light. At least they'll understand us better!"

—**Sy Montgomery, bestselling author of *How to Be a Good Creature: A Memoir in Thirteen Animals***

"What a pleasure to read [Gwen Cooper's] beautiful stories, brimming with her cat-love and even more important her ability to get you to actually see her cats . . . You will want to see more and more. She can become your next obsession, as she has become mine!"

—**Jeffrey Moussaieff Masson, international bestselling author of *The Nine Emotional Lives of Cats***

Praise for *Love Saves the Day*

"Prudence is a sassy but sensitive feline heroine."

—**Time**

"Once again Gwen Cooper shines her light on the territory that defines the human/animal bond."

—**Jackson Galaxy, star of *My Cat From Hell***

"Hauntingly beautiful, heart touching, and at times painfully raw. This book will stay with you long after you turn the final page."

—**The Conscious Cat**

Also by Gwen Cooper

Homer's Odyssey: A Fearless Feline Tale, or How I Learned About Love and Life with a Blind Wonder Cat

Homer and the Holiday Miracle

Spray Anything: More True Tale of Homer & the Gang

My Life in a Cat House: True Tales of Love, Laughter, and Living with Five Felines

The 10th Anniversary Homer's Odyssey Scrapbook

PAWSOME! Head Bonks, Raspy Tongues & 101 Reasons Why Cats Make Us So, So Happy

YOU are PAWSOME! 75 Reasons Why Your Cats Love You, and Why Loving Them Back Makes You a Better Human

The Homer Chronicles

GWEN COOPER

HOMER: THE NINTH LIFE OF A BLIND WONDER CAT

and

SPRAY ANYTHING: MORE TRUE TALES OF HOMER AND THE GANG

Cooper, Gwen.
The Homer chronicles: Homer: the ninth life of a blind wonder cat and spray anything: more true tales of Homer and the gang
ISBN 979-8-9867722-4-0
Nonfiction; memoir; pets

Contents

GWEN COOPER

Homer

THE NINTH LIFE OF A
BLIND WONDER CAT

The Sequel to the *New York Times* Bestseller *Homer's Odyssey*

Foreword

I'VE BEEN WRESTLING WITH the idea of writing a sequel to *Homer's Odyssey* for nearly two years now—feeling, on the one hand, that there were certainly more Homer stories to be told; but, on the other hand, that to make something "book length" would require adding an awful lot of padding. *Homer's Odyssey* was published in 2009 and covered the first twelve years of Homer's life. Homer lived to be sixteen, and so a new book would have significantly less ground to cover.

What you are holding now is the solution I eventually reached—what I like to call a "mini-sequel," roughly one- third the length of the original. Not as long as many books, perhaps, but (I think) exactly the length it needs to be.

Length wasn't my only concern. I can't speak for other writers, but for me, to write about something is to relive it as vividly as I did the first time around. I don't know how to make a reader see and feel things that I'm not seeing and feeling myself at the moment

I'm writing about them. There were many, many wonderful times with Homer during those four years after *Homer's Odyssey* came out, and you'll read those stories here. But there were also some hard times when we lost him, and I wasn't sure I could bear to go through them again.

Well, it wasn't the first time I've been wrong, and it won't be the last. One of the cruelest things about losing a loved one is the way that time makes our memories fade— until what remains isn't the substance of something, only the factual knowledge that it once existed. But, in writing this book, I've gotten to live with Homer again. I've gotten to feel his little head pushing hard into my hand as he demanded his daily pettings; to hear the distinctive *clip-clip* of his feet as he followed me down the hall; and to listen once more to the very specific melodic bird-song that ran beneath his purr. It's a sound I would instantly know from any other cat's purr, even if I were blindfolded.

The only thing that seems remarkable now is that I'd ever thought I was losing those things. And the only regret I have is that it's taken me so long to write my way back to them. I've spent the last weeks feeling Homer with me— the substance of him, a physical presence—as I haven't gotten to do in far too long.

That's the gift this book has given me. What I hope it will give to readers is more Homer, of course, more of the happy times they shared with us and loved in reading the first book, and all the comedy of seeing a little blind housecat— who, once upon a time, nobody else had wanted—take the world by storm.

I also hope that it will help bring clarity to some of the issues that we wrestled with—elder care and end-of-life issues that all animal guardians will have to face eventually. Medical treatment for animals has come a long way since I was a kid living in a family filled with rescue dogs. Often the question now isn't, *What* can *we do?* but, *What* should *we do?* How much money is too much to spend? How much aggressive medical care is justifiable, even if it's the only way to prolong a beloved cat's life?

There's no one right answer to these questions— although in this Foreword (and only in the Foreword), I'd like to float the idea of pet health insurance for anyone who knows they wouldn't be able to come up with, say, five thousand dollars in cash or credit at a moment's notice (which is probably most of us). The monthly premiums are very reasonable and, as they say, you can't put a price tag on peace of mind.

I was lucky as my cats grew older, in that whatever money I had, I'd earned by writing about *them*. I also didn't have children or a mortgage. So whether I could find the money for their care, and whether it was "prudent" to spend that money on them, weren't really questions. If the money came from them, then how could I not give it back?

Nevertheless, we ended up making very different decisions for Vashti, Scarlett, and Homer—because they were three very different cats. Vashti was easygoing and could handle whatever the doctors wanted to do, so we let them throw the whole arsenal at her. Scarlett was a surly girl and almost morbidly dignified, so we opted for a middle course—surgery for her cancer, but not chemotherapy or the removal (at the age of nearly seventeen) of her affected leg.

And Homer...well, Homer was Homer. He knew his own mind. He also knew his own strength—better, as it turned out, than even I did.

Certainly better than his doctors did.

And I have no doubt that when the kittens we adopted in 2012—whose antics, exploits, and hero-worship adoration of Homer you'll also read in these pages— become senior kitties someday, the decisions we make for them and with them will be different as well. Clayton and Fanny are as much one-of-a-kind individuals as our other cats ever were.

One last thought before moving on: Animals are luckier than humans, because animals get to live in the *now*. They do not fear death, or torment themselves with questions about what comes after. No cat has ever desperately hoped for one more year of life so she can finally see Paris, finish her memoirs, or watch her grandchildren graduate from high school. I genuinely believe that, if our animals could understand such things and talk to us about them, they wouldn't want us to spend ourselves into bankruptcy for the sake of trying to stretch fifteen years into sixteen, or even six years into twelve.

Cats know when they feel happy, when they feel comforted, and when they feel loved. None of us ever knows how much time we'll have, and you weren't put in your cat's life to guarantee him a certain minimum number of years. You were put in his life to provide him with happiness, comfort, and love. If you have given your cat (or dog, or bunny, or horse, or guinea pig) a life built on these things, then you've done your job, and you've done it perfectly. And the moment you put all those things in jeopardy is the moment you'll know you've gone too far.

It will be hard to know these things in the chaos of that moment in which they're happening, when decisions have to be made. I know that firsthand. But if you pause for a moment, take a deep breath, and listen to your cat, he will tell you.

I've spent *far* more time discussing this here than I do in the book itself. First and foremost, this is a book of stories—stories about a cat who rose from obscurity to fame, who was promoted from barely tolerated baby brother to adored "big kid," and who continues to save the lives of other animals to this day, simply because *he* lived and his story was told.

Thank you for the gift of letting me tell these stories— and for the additional, greater gift of keeping Homer alive. As long as there is you, there will be him.

Gwen Cooper
New York, NY
November 26, 2015

"Cat Lovers Don't Read Books"

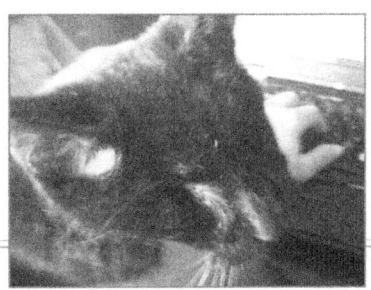

There is no accounting for luck; Zeus gives prosperity to rich and poor just as he chooses, so you must take what he has seen fit to send you and make the best of it.
-HOMER, *The Odyssey*

FAMOUS CATS WEREN'T A *thing* like they are today, back when I first began writing the proposal and outline for *Homer's Odyssey* in 2007. There were no cat cafes. Cat videos hadn't yet taken over the internet. The "Friskies 50" list of the internet's fifty most influential cats was years away not only from execution, but from any relevance. Everybody knew about famous animated cats, like Felix, Tom, Sylvester, the Aristocats, and the perennial Hello Kitty. I remembered a movie from childhood called *That Darn Cat!* There were celebrity cats like Morris and the elegant Fancy Feast Persian, although they were "played" by a succession of different cats, more brand icons than actual felines. A fictional kitty named Sneaky Pie Brown starred in a series of cozy mystery novels. But there didn't seem to be any real-life famous cats, cats who were also members of real-life human families.

There was, however, a cat I'd read about in a recent newspaper article—a cat who'd lived in a library in small- town Iowa, and whose human caregiver had just sold a proposal for a book about his life for more than a million dollars.

My own first book, a novel about South Beach, had been published a few months earlier. Now I was trying to figure out a second book. I didn't think I could earn anything close to a million dollars for any book idea I might have, but I remember putting down the newspaper and looking across the living room at Homer—who was, at the time, visible only from the waist down, the upper half of his body buried under the sofa as he struggled to retrieve an intriguing new belled toy that had rolled away from him—and thinking, *I'll bet I could write a book about Homer. Homer's a pretty cool cat...*

Once I had the idea, I couldn't shake it loose—as if it had always been waiting there for me to unearth. Over the next few weeks, I started jotting down notes and writing out some preliminary paragraphs. I was still working full- time in an office, so I wrote in the pre-dawn hours of early morning—hours when Homer himself was the most active, sparking ideas and connections to half-forgotten memories of our earliest life together. Mornings were when Homer was likeliest to decide to use the toilet instead of the litter- box, to chase his big sisters down the hall (*Wait up, you guys!*), or to disrupt my writing with a preemptory head- bonk as he sat down smack in the middle of the computer keyboard, leaving me to wonder for the millionth time how a blind cat—just like any "normal" cat—infallibly *knew* when I was looking at a book or a newspaper or a computer screen, at anything rather than at him, and made up his mind to put an immediate end to *that*.

At the end of two months, I had enough written down to show my L.A.-based literary agent. He was decidedly underwhelmed by the whole thing. Those who've read the

Afterword to the paperback edition of *Homer's Odyssey* may recall that his initial response was, "But why would anybody want to *read* this?"

"Because a lot of people like cats?" I'd been so flummoxed by his question that I heard myself phrasing my answer—a statement I knew for a fact to be true—as if it, too, were a question, the answer to which I was unsure of. "Because Homer is blind and interesting and has an inspirational life story?"

My agent was blunt. "The writing is there, but I don't think it's a good idea. I wouldn't be able to take it to editors."

I didn't just pay my agent to make deals for me—I also paid him for his career advice. He knew the publishing industry better than I did, and choosing to move forward with my blind-cat book against that advice was easier said than done.

I took to Google, trying to get a sense of how many others like me there might be out there—people who were also living with blind and "special-needs" cats. I ended up calling a woman named Alana Miller, who ran an organization called Blind Cat Rescue in North Carolina. We talked for a while about the plight of blind cats, the barriers they faced in finding adoptive homes, the way so many were summarily euthanized in open-intake shelters. We

agreed—perhaps idealistically, but with utter sincerity— that if a book like this could save even one of them, it would be worth the effort of having written it.

I'd already been working with the notion of *blind leaps of faith* as being one of the central themes of this embryo book, and I decided to take one now. *Thank you so much for everything you've done for me, and for being the first person to have confidence in me as a writer,* I wrote to my agent a few days later. *But we see my proposed HOMER'S ODYSSEY project so very differently that I believe it's in our mutual best interests to part ways.*

I didn't know many other writers who could refer me to their agents, so I went back to what I had done to find my first one—sending blind query letters and emails "over the transom" (meaning without a referral from another client). But this time I didn't have to wait close to a year to hear back, as I had with the first book. Within only a few weeks, a senior agent with a prestigious New York literary agency pronounced herself intrigued by both the writing and the story as I'd outlined it, despite being a self- professed "dog person." My confidence was bolstered by this—that I wasn't just getting the, *Awwwwww...Homer's a cute kitty!* endorsement—and also by how quickly I'd found an agent this time. Surely, I told myself, this could only auger good things. The two of us spent the next four or five months working together closely on an outline, a full proposal, and two sample chapters. We went back and forth over whether those sample chapters should simply be the first two chapters—or perhaps the story of Homer chasing off the burglar? Passages about Homer catching flies in mid-air? Homer and his Kleenex guitar? Final decisions were eventually made, and it was just after Memorial Day of 2008 when we decided we were ready to share *Homer's Odyssey*—at least in its broad strokes—with others.

It may have taken months to pull the proposal together, but it took only a few weeks for the rejections to start coming in from publishers. *The writing is wonderful, and I'd love to see more from this author,* the typical rejection would begin. *But in a crowded pet-memoir marketplace, I just don't feel that Homer is interesting enough to stand out.*

"Crowded marketplace?!" I'd exclaim to my agent. The only other cat memoir at the time was the one about Dewey, the Iowa library cat, and that hadn't even come out yet.

Ironically, Homer would usually be doing something that I thought was very interesting—or, at a minimum, entertaining—whenever one of these letters would come in. I remember that when I got the first one, Homer had just "liberated" a bag full of catnip toys I'd recently stocked up on. I'd double-wrapped the toys in two plastic bags, hidden those bags inside a duffle bag, and secreted the whole thing underneath a mound of clothes in the bottom of the closet, so that I could distribute them one at a time as the old ones wore out, without the cats' pestering me to death. But Homer's unerring nose had found them anyway. He'd burrowed assiduously into that mound of clothes intended for the laundry—kicking dirty socks and underwear into a heedless pile on the floor behind him—unzipped the duffel bag with his teeth and claws, and torn through the first plastic bag. Looking for all the world like Santa Claus (Santa Claws?), Homer now pranced down the hall and into the living room with the sack of toys between his teeth, the other two cats for once following *him* eagerly as they waited for him to distribute the booty.

"Not *interesting* enough?!" Poor Laurence, then my husband-to-be, was generally the only receptacle for my indignation, which waxed hot when I'd receive one of these letters. "*The cat has no eyes!* Does he need to have no eyes and also learn how to juggle?" I'd demand. "Would that make them happy? Maybe if Homer had no eyes *and* could ask for his food in perfect sign language like Koko the gorilla."

That Homer wasn't "interesting" enough (or some variation
of that) was what my agent and I heard most frequently. Also
that animal lovers only wanted to read books about dogs and
horses; that animal lovers didn't want to read animal books at
all in "our current tech-centric environment;" that animal lovers
were only receptive to picture books. One editor informed us matter-of-factly that "cat lovers don't read books." *Why do you think
there aren't more cat books?* he asked with perfect *Catch-22* logic.
Another said that, sure, maybe cat lovers read books, but they
didn't read memoirs. A third was confident that while cat lovers
might read books—and while some of those books might even be
memoirs—they definitely didn't read *cat* memoirs. (I wish I could
say I was making this stuff up.)

By now, I had lost my job as a marketing executive at a magazine
company, which had been acquired by another magazine company
and then dissolved. The crux of my job had been the analysis of
market research on our readers' consumer-spending habits. The
"Marketing Analysis" section I'd written for the *Homer's Odyssey*
proposal had been exhaustive. I'd provided data on the percentage
of cat- owning U.S. households (roughly one third—or, expressed
another way, around one hundred million Americans living with
at least one cat); the amount of money spent per year by those
households on cat-related products and services; and, specifically,
the higher-than-average propensity of a wide swath of the U.S.
cat-owning population to spend their disposable income on enter-
tainment-related purchases, including dinners out, movie tickets,
and books.

"If there's any hard data out there," I'd say to Laurence, "supporting the thesis that 'cat lovers don't read books,' I'd be pretty
darn interested in seeing it." (I'm afraid I generally used a saltier
word than *darn.* Forgive me. Those were dark days.)

At this point, our wedding was only a couple of months off, and I was starting to panic. It's all well and good to get married for richer or poorer, but it still feels awful to enter your marriage without a job or prospects or any viable means of earning an income. Homer was recovering from a recent health scare, the treatment of which had not only eaten into my finances, but had taken its emotional

toll on us both. As much as I tried rationally to dismiss the idea, I had the persistent feeling that Homer had gotten sick *because* I wanted to write about him—that my hubris in thinking ours a story worth sharing publicly had been met by the powers that be with a not-so-gentle rebuke. I was supposed to cherish Homer as he was, the private heart of our own home, and be grateful for that.

It was when things seemed bleakest that I got an electrifying phone call from my agent. A large publishing imprint—one of the biggest and most venerable in the industry—was interested in *Homer's Odyssey.* Not only were they interested, they wanted to meet with me in person—along with my agent, a couple of senior editors, the group publisher, and various vice presidents in publicity and marketing. Then my agent said the words that every author dreams of hearing: "They're talking about a six- figure advance."

Six figures! Between my unemployed status and upcoming wedding, money was tight. Still, in the week I had before that meeting, I went out and bought a new outfit. I got my hair professionally blown out at a fancy SoHo salon. I invested in a forty-dollar manicure and sixty-dollar pedicure at a high-end spa in the Meatpacking District, rather than relying on the eight-dollar manicures I usually got from an elderly Chinese woman in our apartment building. (I was convinced that senior-level publishing muckety-mucks would be able to tell the difference.) I spent an hour carefully applying my makeup, so it would look like I wasn't wearing any. I even sprang for a hired car service to take me to the meeting, afraid of relying on the vagaries of afternoon cab availability to get me there on time.

I was already in the car and on my way uptown when I got the call from my agent. Everything had been cancelled. The group publisher (the big boss, basically) hadn't known what the book was about until shortly before the meeting was supposed to begin. She'd never heard of anything as "creepy" as a cat without eyes, and she was appalled that anyone on her team had considered acquiring *Homer's Odyssey*. There was a rumor afloat that she'd gone so far as demoting the senior editor who'd first read the proposal and recommended it for acquisition—as an example to others never to let anything this awful cross her desk again.

"*Homer's Odyssey* now has an official body count," I told Laurence grimly that night, when he got home from work and asked how my meeting had gone.

I'm not sure which hurt worse—the brutality of that last-minute cancellation, after a week of raised hopes and what now seemed like a pathetic level of over-preparation. Or hearing poor Homer, tiny Homer who'd never done a mean thing to anyone in his life, described as "creepy."

And whose fault is that? I asked myself. Who had subjected Homer to the mockery and derision of ignorant strangers?

I had. I had done it. And even though I knew Homer had no idea that anything unkind had been said about him— or even that such a thing as unkind words existed—those words had opened a wound right in my heart. It hadn't taken much to revive fears I'd had years ago—the sense that it was my job to safeguard Homer in the disability I'd long- since stopped thinking of that way, to protect him against people who wouldn't understand him, or who would say ugly things merely because he was different.

Homer didn't know why he, along with Scarlett and Vashti, unexpectedly found tuna mixed in with their dinner that night. He didn't know why I cuddled him closer on the couch before going to bed. He merely purred with contentment, nuzzling his head into the crook of my neck as he drifted off to sleep.

Technically, this hadn't been the final word. There were still a few more editors we hadn't heard back from. It was possible that one of them might decide to give *Homer's Odyssey* a shot.

But I knew I was finished with the whole business. It was one thing to take a blind leap of faith. It was quite another to bang your head—your own and the heads of the ones you loved—repeatedly against the same brick wall, with nothing to show for it but lumps. As soon as I returned from my honeymoon, I vowed, I would send out résumés and look for a proper job.

I got married two weeks later, and drifted through my wedding day as serene as if everything had already been settled. As far as I was concerned, it had.

LAURENCE AND I WERE married on September 13, 2008, and left for our honeymoon the next evening. And while we spent the following week lolling on Bahamian beaches, enjoying those first few days of married life, the world fell apart.

We returned to find that what would eventually be called the Great Recession had kicked off in our absence. The job I'd been sure I would land, once I devoted my time to looking, now seemed a dubious proposition at best. Nobody was hiring.

So, when I got an email from my agent a week after our return, I saw things in a much different light than I had right before the wedding. An editor named Caitlin Alexander at Delacorte, a Random House imprint, wanted to acquire *Homer's Odyssey*. After a few days of back-and-forth with my agent over numbers, they made us an offer— not the million-plus dollars the book about Dewey had sold for, but enough to cover my rent and, if I was thrifty, basic living expenses for a year. Even better than the money was Caitlin herself—kind and cat-loving but also sharp, with ideas for improving my outline that were so insightful, I was excited at the prospect of working with her.

It was Homer who gave Caitlin the final seal of approval, the night she came to our apartment for dinner. "So this is *Homer*," she said, when Homer made his usual appearance at the front door to greet the new person. There was a kind of reverence in the way she said his name, a tone that previously Homer had only been used to hearing in *my* voice, and he responded to it immediately. Caitlin crouched down and placed one of her hands beneath his nose for him to sniff. But Homer was far more interested in the cat treats she'd brought and now held in the other. One paw reached up delicately to swipe them onto the floor, where he greedily gobbled them up. Once all the treats had been dispatched, Homer placed both front paws on Caitlin's knee, so he could raise himself up and sniff her more thoroughly—obviously hoping for more treats. Caitlin was enraptured, answering Laurence and me in an absent-minded way when we spoke, wholly preoccupied with watching Homer.

"Would you like a glass of wine, Caitlin?" I asked.

"Hmmm...?" Caitlin was scratching Homer beneath his chin, fascinated with watching the muscles around the place where his eyes would have been relax in pleasure. "Sure, that sounds good."

"Red or white?"

Homer had now flopped onto the floor and rolled halfway onto his back, delighted with the attention as Caitlin continued to stroke his chin and neck. "Oh... whichever. Hey, look how well he gets around!" she exclaimed, as Homer—deciding he'd received enough pettings for now, and realizing that no further treats were immediately forthcoming—walked off to find something more entertaining to do. "Look how he knows exactly where his toys are! And he doesn't bump into anything!"

Scarlett and Vashti observed all this from the sidelines with a kind of harrumph-y disdain. *What's so interesting?* they seemed to be asking themselves. *It's just* Homer, *for crying out loud. We manage not to bump into things all the time.*

Although we didn't know it at the time, this would become a sort of template for the way many encounters would play out in our home over the next year.

The paperwork for *Homer's Odyssey* was finalized in late October of 2008, and the book was scheduled for publication in late August of 2009. It seemed a long way off. But to make that publication date, I would have to write the entire book by the end of January. I buckled down, and by working fifteen-hour days I managed to have my complete first draft written and submitted by Monday, February 2.

Homer would have his first professional photo shoot later that same day.

By then, the book about Dewey the Library Cat had finally "pubbed," and it had been a big hit. Suddenly, the conventional wisdom on whether or not there was a market for cat memoirs had shifted. Between that and the success of *Marley and Me,* pet memoirs were the hot new thing. And what had begun as the small passion project of one cat- loving editor had now become worthy of the full weight of Delacorte's serious attention.

I had taken numerous photos of Homer when I'd first started working on the book proposal, in order to submit them along with the writing. They had been deemed "just darling" by Caitlin, although of course none of them were of the professional caliber required to grace the cover of a book Delacorte hoped might be one of its bigger Fall '09 titles. A professional photographer was therefore dispatched to our apartment with all due haste—and an entirely new phase in our lives began.

People who came to see us had always been interested in Homer. He was (the opinion of certain editors notwithstanding) an interesting little guy. But now began an influx of visitors who were *only* interested in Homer. My day would come eventually, further down the road, when it was time to do in-studio radio spots or phone interviews for newspapers and magazines. I was fated to become one of the luckiest "cat ladies" ever—because people *wanted* to hear me talk about my cat! At length! Sometimes for as long as an hour at a stretch!

The focus for now, however, was on turning Homer into a star. You've probably heard that stars aren't born, they're made. Well, I'm here to tell you that it's true. Behind every star is an entire team of people invisible to the public. Not just the photographers, the editors, the lighting assistants, the stylists (or, in the case of a cat, professional groomers—although they learned quickly that *our* star strongly preferred *not* to have anyone but mom trim his claws or touch his paws, thank you very much). There are also managers, publicists, "stage moms," personal assistants, gatekeepers, and lackeys whose job it is to keep the star happy and engaged, to get him out of his trailer in time for the shoot and in a suitable emotional state to work, to run and fetch whatever the star may want to eat or amuse himself with.

When it came to making Homer a star, all of those latter roles were filled by me—with an occasional assist from Laurence, who these days was working from home. (The L.A.-based entertainment magazine where he was an editor hadn't laid off staff yet, but they had sent their Manhattan-based employees to work at home, so they could liquidate their New York office—which we took to be an ominous sign.) Laurence, however, would usually clear out for the day whenever our apartment was taken over for video or photo shoots.

"Managing" Homer soon became my full-time job. It was my responsibility to set his appointments; thoroughly brush and groom him ahead of time, so that his coat would shine with a high gloss and without any pesky stray bits of fur that might dangle from his haunches and ruin a shot; to make sure he got plenty of rest before a shoot began; to keep us stocked up on the tuna, turkey, and toys required to keep him engaged, happy, and playful; to wrangle him from spot to spot as the daylight or whims of whoever was shooting him changed.

I had to pop open cans of tuna when they wanted Homer to raise his head and perk up his ears; to dip toys and crumpled pieces of paper and bits of sisal rope in the tuna oil when Homer's interest in them flagged and he'd start to trot over to me. *Why aren't you playing with any of this cool stuff, mom?* I had to gauge when it was finally time for Homer to retire to the sanctity of his cat tree for a quick, replenishing cat nap. I'd gently suggest to whoever was in charge that Homer really *could* use a bit of time to himself—at which point he or she would cry, "That's lunch, everybody!" and the cameramen, the sound crew (if it was a video shoot), the lighting techs, the groomer and stylist, the field producer, and the field producer's assistant would ask me to recommend a nearby restaurant. And would I mind terribly calling ahead for a reservation, since they'd need a large table?

It was my job to do all these things and more and then...to get out of the shot.

I used to joke that my name might as well officially be changed to Gwen "Thank You Now Please Get Out Of The Shot" Cooper. "We'd like to shoot Homer in front of the bookcase—he looks adorable with all those books behind him! Thank you so much [after I'd lured Homer to the desired spot with a cheerful, *Come on, Homer-Bear!*]... but could you move juuuuuuust a little to the left? A little more? We can still see part of your arm."

Or, "I'd like to get Homer in front of the window. He'll be majestic with the Manhattan skyline behind him. Could you get him to...yes...perfect, that's it! But your hair is so curly and it's interfering with Homer's light—could you maybe pull it back?"

Far be it for me to interfere with Homer's light!

If Homer had been a different kind of a cat—a cat like Scarlett, for example—all the "managing" in the world couldn't have made these shoots possible. But Homer had always liked attention, and the people who gave it to him. He was intriguing not just because of his blindness, but because he had real charisma.

That might sound like an odd word to apply to a cat. Charisma, though, is little more than the ability of some people (or cats) to make you feel—even if only for the span of a few minutes—as if *you* are the most fascinating thing going, the very person they'd been hoping to get to spend time with.

Homer had that ability in spades.

Every strange person who came to our home and crawled on their belly holding a camera before them—so as to shoot Homer at his own level—was one more friend for him to make, one more cheerful greeting for him to bestow, receiving a playful scratch behind his ears in return. Scarlett and Vashti ran for the hills whenever our apartment was thus inundated, but Homer could never get over how much cool *stuff* these people brought with them! Cartons and crates, lighting reflectors, boom mics, duffel bags for Homer to crawl in, around, and over. His nose and whiskers would twitch non-stop as he tried to process all the exotic new smells of equipment bags that had been on airplanes, in studios and out on location shoots, perhaps even (in the case of the crew from Animal Planet) in the homes of other cats.

Homer relaxing in his "trailer" between takes

The camera crews came to our home as a team of seen-it-all professionals, out on just another job—and an annoying one at that, because what could be more irritating (or less interesting) than working with a *cat?*—but they left as an adoring cult. Like my former boyfriends of old, who'd proudly proclaimed, *Homer's my buddy!*, each photographer and videographer was convinced that he or she had formed a unique and special bond with Homer over the course of the shoot, that some magical *thing* had happened between the two of them during those few hours they had together.

Homer could make you feel that way. He seemed to know precisely when they wanted him to sit still as a statue and look majestic, to chase around toys in goofy, kittenish fashion, to run or jump or flip around on his back with un-self-conscious abandon, to turn his head shyly a little to the side, as if to say, *I'm strong, but also vulnerable.* Maybe he even *did* know. Homer was a sensitive cat, one who'd always paid close attention to the people around him. He had ways of knowing things that even I couldn't account for.

Do you see this?, they'd demand. *Do you see how he's responding to me?* Click-click, the camera would go. *He's a great cat, Gwen, a really exceptional cat.* And then they'd remind me, for the umpteenth time to, please, get out of the shot.

I knew that I hovered. Part of it was my old over-protectiveness, which reared up again and was hard to suppress as I watched strangers cluster around Homer, amidst walls of gear five times his size. As for Homer himself, he was almost never nervous with all the activity going on around him. All he needed to find these unprecedented new experiences completely enjoyable was the knowledge that I was somewhere nearby. But with so much going on—with so many people and so much equipment crammed within the relatively small space of our living room—it was difficult for him to catch my scent if I wasn't standing close. Speaking to him in a reassuring voice wasn't a great option, as it tended to cause him to leave off whatever he'd been doing and head in my direction.

As soon as Homer wasn't sure I was there anymore— when the horrifying thought that I might have left him *alone* with all these strangers appeared to cross his mind—then he was capable of being as uncooperative as any irate star. The fur on his back would start to rise, he'd twist his head wildly in un-shoot-able postures, nose in the air as he tried to figure out my location. I'd rush over to pet him and smooth down his fur. *I'm not going anywhere, Homer-Bear. I'm right here with you.* Thus calmed and restored to cheerful good humor, Homer would once again return to the work at hand as if he'd been born to do it.

And I, of course, would hasten to get out of the shot.

ALL TOLD, THERE WERE only perhaps seven or eight of these shoots, stretched out over nearly as many months. But they loomed so large with their strangeness and excitement that they cast long shadows. As the count-down to *Homer's Odyssey*'s publication date began, and as the anxiety and anticipation continued to build, it was hard to feel that our lives were quite what they had been only a few months ago—although it was equally hard to say just what, exactly, they were becoming.

Some of these shoots were arranged by my publisher for their own purposes—two sessions in our home in order to get the ideal cover shot of Homer (as well as extras to be used inside the book itself), and one at an off-site photographer's studio for additional publicity shots of Homer and me together. I talked about that one in the

Afterword for *Homer's Odyssey*—the near impossibility of wrangling Homer in an unfamiliar space, trying to get him to stay still long enough to have his picture taken. All Homer himself wanted to do was explore this new place and introduce himself to all the new people within it. It was so *very* hard to get him to sit still that, as I noted in the Afterword, eventually the photographer and lighting techs unhooked all the equipment from its various stands and carried it by hand, so they could follow Homer wherever he went. As long as I live, I'll never forget the sight of a team of professionals—and one hovering stage mom— following along behind a blind cat in parade-like fashion, crying, *Wait! I think he's going* this *way now!*

People magazine wanted photos of Homer for insets to accompany the full-page review of the book they planned to run. *Ladies Home Journal* was going to excerpt a portion of *Homer's Odyssey*—from the chapter describing the night Homer had chased off the burglar—in their September issue. For this shoot, along with the usual crew they also sent over to our apartment a hair-and-make-up person and wardrobe stylist for me. They wanted shots of Homer and me together to accompany the piece—shots of Homer lying on my chest, shots of Homer in my arms, shots of Homer nuzzling my ear. In the end, though, they ran a photo of just Homer by himself.

"The problem," as I would later observe to a friend, when the issue came out and I saw that I wasn't in it, "is that I didn't get out of the shot."

Animal Planet did a segment on Homer for their *Cats 101* show. The segment was only a few minutes long, but it took a grueling eight hours to get all the footage they needed. Even Homer was spent by the end of the day, when our apartment was in shambles and all he wanted was to use his litter-box without having a cameraman closely following his movements. At one point, he turned with an indignant hiss on the cameraman, who followed behind him with dogged persistence. *Do you mind? I'm trying to pee in privacy!* I will say, though, that nobody we worked with knew how to record cats more unobtrusively than the Animal Planet crew. They were even able to capture the notoriously camera-shy Vashti and Scarlett, and there was no way any of us would have made it through a day that long without their expertise.

The coverage for *USA Today* happened in three waves. The books editor—the person who decided which books *USA Today* would cover; which of their various staff and freelance reviewers would be assigned to cover them; and who also wrote the revered-within-the-industry "Book Buzz" column, which a month earlier had decreed that, "*Homer's Odyssey* will be huge," causing bookstore pre-orders to quintuple overnight—was also a cat lover. ("So much for cat lovers not reading books," I told my agent.). She wanted to do more with *Homer's Odyssey* than simply have it reviewed, and she came over to our apartment to interview me personally—although I didn't kid myself that so high-ranking a personage would have gone to all the trouble of coming to me if she hadn't wanted to meet Homer as well.

Homer seemed almost relieved when someone came to our home wanting only to sit and chat, rather than putting him through his paces. He curled up in my lap for most of the interview, drowsy and comfortable as the editor reached out from time to time to stroke his head. "He really is a loving little guy, isn't he," she observed, and Homer rewarded this by pushing his entire face into her hand, his way of demanding that she rub him harder. For once, even Scarlett and Vashti ventured out, eager to feast upon the cat treats I'd scattered around liberally as a way of ensuring that Homer would stay in the living room throughout the interview and not head off to his "trailer"—i.e. the little cave in his cat tree.

Homer, however, was more interested in the editor than in the treats, having had so many in recent weeks that he was becoming ever-so-slightly bored with them. (Ah, the ennui of stardom!)

A day later, a photographer from *USA Today* came to shoot Homer for the story—one lone photo-journalist and his camera, without all the rigging and light reflectors and duffle bags we'd become accustomed to. I was so used to being asked to...you know...get out of the shot that I was wearing work clothes, the hair I'd washed but hadn't bothered styling that morning (because who cared what *I* looked like?) pulled back in an untidy ponytail. But the books editor had instructed the photographer to shoot

Homer and me together—which is why, to my everlasting shame, Homer and I were immortalized in the pages of the nation's biggest newspaper with me looking like I'd just finished moving furniture.

Homer, it goes without saying, looked sleek and shiny and impossibly perfect.

The day after *that*, a *USA Today* videographer arrived to film me reading an excerpt of *Homer's Odyssey* while Homer scampered in the background, planning to post the video to the *USA Today* website and YouTube channel once the book had been released. I'd invested in a brand-new catnip toy for the occasion, in order to ensure maximum frolicking. Homer systematically demolished that toy over the course of the hour it took us to shoot, tearing it to shreds and releasing all the catnip into a giant mound in front of him, which he then rolled and flipped around in while his entire face became encrusted with 'nip—until he looked like Al Pacino at the end of *Scarface*. The catnip made Homer talkative, and so that footage is one of the very few recordings in existence that captured the sound of Homer's own voice—and, for that reason, I treasure it to this day.

Perhaps the craziest day was when we recorded the book trailer—the promotional video commissioned by my publisher for placement on YouTube and various other websites. They'd taken over a two-bedroom suite at the Hotel Pennsylvania for the shoot, across the street from Madison Square Garden, where many a visiting rocker had stayed and partied back in the hotel's glory days.

They sent a town car to pick Homer and me up. Homer had been reluctant to get into his carrier, and it was raining as I dashed as quickly as I could from apartment building to car—although Homer did catch a few drops, which didn't improve his mood. The driver helped me load in all the gear I'd thought necessary to bring along if we were going to be shooting out of the house for an entire day—a litter-box and litter, bowls for food and water and food to go in them, a sack of catnip, a bag of Pounce treats, and a large bag of rolling-and-belled toys. I was scheduled for an early-morning arrival—before seven—and I'd requested that as few people as necessary be there when we first arrived, so that Homer would have time to acclimate to a new place before it was time for the hair-and-makeup person to go to work on me, and the groomer to go to work on him.

There was a single cameraman there to greet us when we knocked on the door of the suite. He'd beaten us to the hotel by only an hour, having just arrived on a red-eye from L.A. for the purpose of recording Homer's first hour of exploration. I set up food and water bowls for Homer in the kitchen, and placed the litter-box there as well, setting Homer in the litter-box first—as was our custom when I brought him to a new place—so that he wouldn't have to wonder where it was.

"I've never seen such big aural canals in a cat," the cameraman noted. "You can see all the way down into his ears. They're huge!"

"Homer's hearing is off the charts," I agreed, as Homer's head perked up at the sound of my saying his name, and he turned the ears we'd just been discussing in my direction.

"Are you sure he's never been here before?" The cameraman was watching as Homer—nose to the ground— began to figure out the suite and its various rooms. He didn't bump into a single thing, not a wall, not a sofa, not the cabinets in the kitchen or a lamp in the suite's living room. Homer's sensitive nose and remarkable whiskers gave him all the information he needed to navigate seamlessly— just as he'd done time after time in the many homes we'd moved in and out of, back in our earlier years of struggle and constant migration. After about a half-hour of thorough investigation, Homer happily took up play with a catnip ball, fascinated with the way it ricocheted off the bottom of the kitchen cabinets and into the living room. He chased it in and out of bedrooms, under tables, around the sofa and floor lamps, without losing track of it for even a moment.

"I can't believe he's *blind*," the cameraman marveled. "Don't take this the wrong way, but if it weren't for the fact that his eyes are gone, I'd say you were lying."

I laughed. "My husband says the same thing," I told him. "To this day, he swears that Homer's faking blindness."

It was a long day, and the suite began to fill up as the morning wore on. The next to arrive were Homer's and my respective groomers, followed by another cameraman, a lighting tech with trees and enormous reflective panels ("It's hard to get the lighting just right on a black cat," he explained—which I already knew), a sound person with boom mics, a producer, Caitlin, and my publisher's Vice President of Marketing, who had arrived to supervise the shoot personally.

But, with all the primping and preparation, with all the setting up of equipment and moving of furniture, with all the phone calls and consultations and last-minute disagreements about the shot list (which detailed the specific things they wanted to capture Homer doing), it was hours before the shoot proper—wherein I would answer questions about Homer and the book, while Homer did various adorable and active things in the background— even started.

By then, as was his preferred habit on rainy days when thunder rolled with a pleasant far-away rumble beneath the sounds of drops splashing against the windows, Homer wasn't interested in doing anything but napping. He wasn't upset. He was friendly as ever when new people came over to greet him and introduce themselves. He was simply *bored*. All the hoopla over the last few months, all the duffel bags and equipment and strangers and cat treats, all the new toys and the cameras following him to catch his every movement as he sat or ran or stretched or jumped or rolled over, had become old hat. All Homer wanted to do now was sit quietly on the couch behind my head, the way we did on rainy days when we were home alone and I read a book while Homer snoozed peacefully beside me.

Everybody's eyes were on me. But, as every cat person knows, there's only so much you can do with an uncooperative cat. I tried opening a baggie of catnip and wafting it under his nose. Nothing. I tried jangling a belled toy next to his ear. No response.

I got up and walked across the room. "Homer," I cooed. "Homer, come over to mommy."

Homer flicked one ear lazily in the direction of my voice, but didn't stir. *Nah*, he seemed to say. *Don't wanna.*

"Homer-Bear," I sing-songed. I tried rattling a bag of Pounces. "Do you want a treat, Homer? Do you want to come and get a kitty treat, baby boy?"

Homer yawned mightily and extended his front and hind legs in a long, languorous stretch. He flipped onto his back momentarily, then curled back into a ball and continued to nap.

And so, here we were. A room full of people, a crew of professionals who'd flown through the night all the way from the West

Coast, my publisher's Vice President of Marketing (upon whom, I couldn't help but feel, I was making a very bad impression), all the treats and toys any cat would want—all of it here for Homer, and *only* for Homer, and Homer himself couldn't be bothered. He'd already been there. He'd already done that.

"Let me make a call," I told the room, and went to dig my cell out of my purse so I could phone Laurence at home.

"I need you," I told him as soon as he answered. "We need half a pound of that sliced deli turkey Homer likes, and a whole bunch of those little cans of tuna. Do you think you could go to the grocery store and then bring it all here?"

"Yeah, sure."Laurence sounded surprised, but willing to help. "What do you want, Chicken of the Sea?" "No, no." I was beginning to sound frantic. "Not Chicken of the Sea! He likes Bumble Bee, Laurence. *Homer likes Bumble Bee!*"

There was a pause, and then we both began to laugh. We laughed until we were practically crying. Tears ran down my face and my stomach began to ache, making it hard to breathe as I tried to suppress the laughter, aware that all the people in the other room could probably hear me.

Our lives *had* gotten a little crazy. But Homer wasn't some diva, and we weren't his flunkies. Homer was still just *Homer*—the good-natured, high-spirited little boy we fondled and fussed over at home, in private, as soon as the cameras were packed up and gone.

I'd been making myself crazy in part because— yes—I desperately wanted my book to be a success. What author doesn't want that? I knew how incredibly rare it was for a publisher to put this kind of effort and attention into a book, that this particular moment in my life was fleeting and one I needed to enjoy as it was happening, because Homer and I wouldn't be the flavor of the month forever.

But it was more than that. I was also *proud* of Homer—not just of the ease and dignity with which he'd been acquitting himself as all these unusual and unprecedented things were happening to us. I was proud of who he was. I felt entirely vindicated in all the years of faith I'd had in him. And I wanted others to see that. I wanted the whole world to see—naysayers I'd never even met and probably never would, who nevertheless I knew would think, *Why would anybody want a blind cat?* I wanted everybody to view for themselves what a blind cat—*my* blind cat—could do. The veterinarian from whom I'd adopted Homer was writing the Foreword to *Homer's Odyssey*, and I had an idea that some of the people who'd had the chance to adopt him but turned him down, all those years ago, might read this book. They might put two and two together, they might realize what they had discarded as if it were nothing. Their loss had been my infinite gain, but still I wanted them to view Homer with amazement, to read his story with envy and think, *That could have been me.*

And, although I generally didn't consider myself a vindictive person, I wanted to make that one publisher who'd called Homer "creepy" eat her words. I wanted to make her rue the day she'd turned from him in disgust. *I'll show you "creepy,"* I'd say to myself, in steely tones.

Before any of that would happen, however, there was still our immediate problem to contend with—a cat already bored with a fame he technically hadn't attained yet, and the necessity of recapturing his interest just long enough to make it through this last shoot.

"I'll be there as soon as I can with turkey and tuna," Laurence promised, when we had finished laughing.

"*Thank you,*" I told him. "Oh—and make sure it's the fancy albacore. That's his favorite."

Laurence ran out to the grocery store in the rain, waited forever to find a cab—which was always tougher on soggy days like this—and sat in the heavy crosstown traffic for nearly half an hour as he crossed from Second Avenue to where we were waiting at the Hotel Pennsylvania on Seventh. Once he arrived, we had to open a slew of those little cans of tuna before the sound of cans opening and the aroma of fish filling the room intrigued Homer enough to rouse him from his slumber. Laurence went into the suite's kitchen and rattled the paper Homer's favorite turkey was wrapped in, actually going through the motions of making a sandwich until Homer rose languidly from the sofa and trotted into the kitchen to paw at Laurence's leg. *Hey—is that turkey?*

The shoot ran longer than scheduled, but in the end we got the footage of Homer we needed. I took a look at the demolished suite as I was packing up Homer and his gear to head back home. Furniture had been pushed around haphazardly. Lampshades were skewed at odd angles, positioned this way and that to better cast the light onto Homer's black fur. Cameras and lighting reflectors were lying on the floor or leaned against end tables. Nearly two-dozen small, half-opened cans of tuna were scattered on every imaginable surface, along with uneaten bits of turkey strewn across the floor, laid there to tempt Homer into various spots.

I shook my head in amazement as I took it all in, thinking, *Well, I guess we've finally arrived.* Homer had trashed his first hotel room. He was officially a star.

The World's Cat

The Muse brought to the minstrel's
mind a song of heroes whose great fame
rang out under heaven.
-HOMER, *The Odyssey*

HOMER'S ODYSSEY WAS PUBLISHED on August 25, 2009.

I had traveled to Washington, D.C. the night before to do an interview on NPR's "Diane Rehm Show" on the morning of launch, and didn't get back home again until the early evening. Homer spent the night of the book's release feasting on the lobster salad Laurence had prepared for me as a congratulatory surprise, but that I was too wound-up to eat. Scarlett and Vashti didn't care as much for lobster, but Laurence had bought them a tin of fancy canned tuna from our local gourmet shop—which Homer consumed his fair share of as well. I spent the rest of the night refreshing the book's Amazon page every hour, so I could watch as its sales rank rose. (This is something every writer does on the day her book is published, and any writer who tells you she doesn't is totally lying.) Eventually, I moved my laptop computer over to the couch, so I wouldn't have to keep jumping up to see if the numbers had changed. Homer, full of lobster and tuna, snoozed happily beside me.

With all the pre-publication craziness, I'd thought that life would calm down once the book was out. But, soon after it appeared in bookstores, there came a second, smaller wave of press rolling through our apartment in order to meet Homer—the bloggers, vloggers (those with video blogs), and internet radio hosts who hadn't required the longer lead times of magazines and newspapers, and who were thus able to wait until the book was on shelves before planning their coverage.

This second wave of press was much mellower than the first had been, requiring far less of Homer and me. Usually it would just be one person with a hand-held recording device, or perhaps one additional person to hold a video camera. Homer was able to interact with these people with nothing more than his usual level of friendly interest—although I do remember one blogger in particular for whom Homer went absolutely wild.

I had never been nearly as aware of different people's differing smells as Homer was, but this specific blogger had an especially...pungent...aroma that even I could catch from across the room. She smelled strongly of patchouli mixed with insufficiently masked body odor— which is really only worth mentioning because Homer was fascinated by this woman as he'd never been with anyone before, and as I would never see him be with anyone again. It was impossible to keep him off her, to prevent him from crawling up and around her as he tried to take in her scent from all conceivable angles, burying his head in her hair and inserting his nose deeply into more private areas.

"He's certainly a friendly little guy, isn't he?" the blogger observed, trying to angle Homer's nose unobtrusively away from her crotch.

"That he is." I was mortified. "Homer! *Homer! Come...here!*" I spoke in the guttural-voice-through-clenched-teeth tone my own mother had used to rein me in when I was small, whenever my childish high spirits had seemed in danger of causing public embarrassment.

Homer, however, was not to be deterred. "I'm *so* sorry," I apologized. "I don't know what's come over him." Homer's head was still immersed in our guest's nether regions, and finally I went over and lifted him from her, one hand under his breastbone for support while the other took the scruff of his neck in a manner meant to indicate, *I am NOT kidding around!*

But Homer wriggled out of my arms and boomeranged right back to his intrusive examination of every square inch of the blogger's body. "I can put him in the other room, if you'd like," I offered.

"No, don't worry about it!" I may have been appalled at Homer's bad behavior, but the blogger herself seemed unruffled. "But maybe we should open a window?" she added. "Your face looks a little red."

Of all the people who came and went through our home, convinced that during their time with us they'd formed a special bond with Homer unlike anybody else's, this was the one occasion when that was likeliest to be true. There were perhaps a half-dozen or so of these visitors over the course of a couple of days, and then Laurence and I hit the road. Publishers weren't as apt to finance book tours as they'd been once upon a time, but I scheduled a few readings on my own. I did one in New York, of course, where we lived. I did one in L.A. where, after nearly two decades as a film journalist, Laurence had many friends. And I scheduled one in Miami where my parents and some of my old friends still lived. Laurence had given me a necklace to celebrate the book's publication, featuring a tiny cat-shaped pendant made from small black diamonds, and I wore it for luck whenever I made a book- related appearance.

In Miami, I did an in-studio interview at the local NPR station the morning before my reading, and an article about the book and my upcoming appearance was published in the *Miami Herald* the same day. Still, I wasn't expecting much of a turnout beyond my family, my friends, and my parents' friends. Part of the reason why publishers were reluctant to underwrite book tours was because it had become increasingly difficult to get people to turn out for them, even when a book was popular and an author event had been well publicized.

So it was overwhelming to arrive at Books & Books in Coral Gables and find that nearly three hundred people had come. *Three hundred people!* The lead book reviewer for the *Sun-Sentinel*, whose work I'd been reading since I was a teenager, was the one who stepped up to the podium to introduce me, and it was one of the great nights of my life.

I don't think it really hit me until that moment that a *lot* of people were going to read Homer's story. It was one thing to see sales figures projected on a spread sheet, but an entirely different experience to see three hundred individual faces turned my way as I read from the book. There was even a cat in attendance—a tiny blind kitten named Galileo, only a few weeks old, with the two people who'd found him abandoned a few days earlier. They'd brought Galileo to the reading in the hopes that somebody there might be able to help them figure out what to do for him—and, sure enough, representatives from several local rescue groups were on-hand and able to take charge of the situation. (Galileo eventually found a forever home with a reader in Ft. Lauderdale.)

I also realized something else that night that I'd never thought about before—the deep chord that *Homer's Odyssey* would strike in the animal-rescue community. Homer represented any number of cats who rescuers would cry themselves to sleep at night thinking about— cats who were sweet and friendly and loving, cats these rescuers worked with every day, and who they knew would make a wonderful companion to anyone lucky enough to adopt them. But cats (and dogs) who, nevertheless, were consistently passed over for adoption because they were blind, or deaf, or needed extra care for ongoing medical issues, or simply because they had aged out of kitten-hood and were now "too old."

I wasn't the only one who stood vindicated by the publication of Homer's story. And, despite having cared for him for more than twelve years, I wasn't even close to being the one who'd put in the most time and effort— who'd fought the most battles or broken her heart the most often—trying to prove that a special-needs animal was just as capable of loving and being loved as any other, and just as deserving of a chance.

Eight days after *Homer's Odyssey* was published, I received two phone calls—one from Caitlin, and one from the in-house publicist my publisher had assigned to promote *Homer's Odyssey*—both with the same exciting news. After only one week on sale, *Homer's Odyssey* would debut at #14 on the following week's *New York Times* Bestseller List.

Laurence and I celebrated with champagne that night, while Homer, Vashti, and Scarlett were treated to new catnip toys and Homer's beloved deli turkey. When the *New York Times* Book Review in which Homer would be named was finally published, I saw that *Homer's Odyssey* had been called out for special attention in the "Inside the List" feature that ran alongside it. *"Homer's Odyssey* makes its first appearance on the list in 2,720 years," the writer humorously observed, before adding, "Oh, wait! Gwen Cooper's book is actually the story of a tiny blind wonder cat..."

THE NEXT FEW MONTHS were a whirlwind. Although I hadn't been sent on an official book tour, I was invited to speak at shelters and at shelter fundraisers around the country, to advocate for the cause of special-needs animals and of rescue in general.

I hated leaving my three cats as often as I did, traveling more now than I had at any previous time in my life. But, then, I was now firmly self-employed, so when I was home I got to be *home.* My cats and I had never had so many uninterrupted hours in the day together as we did during the times when I wasn't on the road. Homer would greet me with pure delight when I returned from a trip—happy I was back, of course, and also eager to make a thorough investigation of my suitcase and my person.

Every engagement I traveled to included a tour through the shelter where I'd be speaking, along with plenty of cuddling opportunities with the cats that shelter cared for. No matter how thoroughly I showered before getting on a plane, the shoes I wore home and the bag containing clothing I'd worn while away reeked, from Homer's perspective, of other cats. It could take hours for Homer to get through as exhaustive an inspection as he liked, until finally it was time to dump my suitcase contents into the laundry and get them ready for the next trip.

Best of all were the gifts I brought back for the cats. Everywhere I went, people sent me home with gifts for Homer, and I was touched by how many remembered to include Scarlett and Vashti as well—hand-crocheted balls stuffed with catnip, little satin-enclosed catnip pillows with each of the cats' names embroidered on them, hand-knitted and hand-sewn kitty blankets, colorful new bowls for food and water, bags of treats, and noisy playthings, like crinkle balls, by the sack.

Of course it was really Homer, and Homer's story, that everybody was interested in. People wanted to hear live accounts of the tales they'd read in the book, to know how Homer was adjusting to his newfound fame. But Homer couldn't travel or deliver speeches himself, so I went as his proxy. I also did interviews with, and wrote articles for, animal-centric magazines and websites, encouraging the adoption of special-needs animals like Homer. As few "famous cats" as there were at the time, there had never (to my knowledge) been a famous special-needs cat, and so Homer became something of a "poster kitty" for the cause of adopting animals once thought unadoptable. I would eventually hear from people who wrote to say that Homer had inspired them to take a chance on a blind—or otherwise disabled—cat. I can honestly say that I've received no fewer than two hundred of these emails over the past few years, and they're always the greatest letters I get.

I traveled to parts of the country I'd never seen in person before—the Deep South, Texas, the Heartland, the Pacific Northwest, the Rust Belt. I traveled from Minnesota to New Mexico, to Arizona during a heat wave so intense that I could literally feel my *eyeballs* grow warm when I stepped outside. The landscapes would change dramatically each time a plane I was on would land, as would the regional accents, the style of dress, and the local cuisine.

Yet certain things remained constant. I met people of all ages, sizes, religions, and ethnic backgrounds—people who likely would have disagreed vehemently with their counterparts in other regions on everything from politics to place settings (because one would surely consume Alabama hominy grits very differently than Seattle sushi). But the one thing everyone I met agreed about—passionately— was the cause of animal rescue. I can't tell you how many people I've heard, over the last six years, say how

At the Nine Lives Foundation in Redwood City, CA

much better they think animals are than people. But, personally, I think it's that animals bring out the very best in people— until you can't help but realize how ultimately insignificant the rest of the differences are.

Despite my hectic travel schedule of those few months—and despite the fact that those crazy days of video and promotional shoots were essentially over—"managing" Homer was still my full-time job. I had to answer his fan mail, oversee his social media presence, regretfully inform those who wrote to say that they would be vacationing in New York—and could they possibly drop by our place to meet Homer in person?—that, unfortunately, Homer wasn't available for personal appearances. "As if Homer were another New York tourist attraction, like the Statue of Liberty," I would say to Laurence.

And *somebody* had to write the thank-you notes for the many gifts Homer received in the mail—as various and plentiful as the gifts I brought home with me from trips. Scarlett and Vashti got their fair share of the bounty, and may, I think, have enjoyed it even more than Homer did. All the soft kitty blankets—that were just her size!—were a profound joy to Scarlett, who'd always loved anything plush and luxurious. To have something soft and warm to claim for her very own, small enough for her to guard from encroachment by the annoying other cats she was forced to live with, was a gift from above. And Vashti loved catnip even more than Homer did. People sent us catnip they'd grown themselves, on hobby farms or in backyard gardens, and the purity of this home-grown 'nip seemed to make Homer, and especially Vashti, super relaxed and flippy.

For his part, Homer was most enamored of the boxes these gifts came in. He enjoyed them all so much that I couldn't bear to take any away from him—until our living room looked as if we were moving. It was at this point that Laurence tactfully suggested that it might be time to throw at least a few of them away.

As it turned out, there were also quite a few younger readers of *Homer's Odyssey*—elementary and middle- school children who were already passionate about animals, and for whom the message that *different doesn't mean bad* carried more relevance even than it did for adults. One evening, long after the book had been published, a sixth- grade girl came to our apartment with her father, to meet and photograph Homer for an article about him she was writing for *Time For Kids* (*Time* magazine's children's imprint). She took such a grave, shy pleasure in his presence—and Homer was so very gentle with her in his rubbing and head- bonks—that I had to smile at seeing them together.

But well before then I'd been hearing from children of about her age who were writing book reports about Homer and wanted me to answer questions they had about the book, or to know what kids like them could do for other special- needs animals. Sometimes they emailed so they could send me pictures of drawings they'd made of Homer, or of Homer-themed arts-and-crafts projects they'd created for school.

It wasn't just in the U.S. and Canada where Homer was gaining a following. Foreign rights to *Homer's Odyssey* had sold in nearly twenty countries before the book was even published, and some of those translations began to appear right around the time the U.S. edition did. I always got a kick out of the foreign editions, the different artwork of their covers, all the various iterations of Homer that differed so greatly from country to country that it was hard to believe they were all publishing the same book.

Artwork from the Korean edition

Some countries—like Brazil, France, Russia, and China—used the literal translation of "Homer's Odyssey" as the title for their editions. Others took more of a creative license. In Italy it was *Omero Gatto Nero*, in Germany *Homer und Ich*. In Finland, the book was called *Homer – Kissan Uskomaton Elama*, which meant, *Homer – A Cat's Incredible Life*. The Dutch went with a straightforward *Wonderkat!*, and in Hungary it was simply *Homér*—the book's cover a stark block of solid red, with

Homer's name in huge white letters, and in the middle of the cover a very small silhouetted profile of a black cat with a curled tail.

The Japanese title translated roughly into *I See Happy Love.* I'm still unsure as to what the Korean title meant, although I adored the artwork they included. At the end of the book were several pages of prints depicting vividly hued watercolor paintings, like something from a book of fairy tales. One of them showed a girl who I think was supposed to be me—although she looked like *Alice in Wonderland*—being borne aloft into a starry night by a tuxedoed, flower-bearing, eyeless black cat, trailing a little gray tabby and an even smaller white kitty in the air behind her. A smiling man (Laurence?) waved them all off from a bedroom window.

Homer soon began to receive cards and letters and gifts from the other countries where his story had been published. Somewhere along the line, I realized, he had become not merely *my* cat, but the world's cat.

And yet, he was still just our happy little boy. He had been with me for so long—and while I couldn't say that I took him for granted, he had become as essential, yet also as everyday, as the beating of my own heart.

I would look at Homer sometimes—as he chased a bedeviled Scarlett down the hall, or jumped onto my desk and did his best to keep me from typing, or rolled onto his back to groom the chocolate-and-black fur of his belly—and I would marvel. It was an impossible, an incomprehensible, thing to try to fathom, that so many people all across the globe knew him. Knew him and loved him.

NATURALLY, HOMER HAD HIS own Facebook page. It was just a regular personal page at first, but when he reached his 5000-friend limit, I started a "fan" page for him—although I never thought of it that way. Only about a thousand of Homer's Facebook friends followed us to this new page— and even though it grew incrementally, adding perhaps two hundred new followers each month, it still felt like a small, intimate community.

It was Homer's page, and so I wrote there in Homer's voice—not his actual voice, obviously, but the way Homer had always sounded in my own head. I'll admit that I'd never been much for personal photographs, but now we were snapping photos of Homer, Scarlett, and Vashti constantly. I tried to mine our everyday lives for the kinds of things I thought people who'd read the book, and now wanted to keep up with Homer on a day-to-day basis, might find entertaining. *Oh boy! Turkey for dinner!*, I'd write, above a snapshot of Homer doing his best to steal a bit of food from Laurence's plate. Or, *My* little bag of catnip! MINE! along with a photo of Homer crouched protectively over one of the small bags of home-grown 'nip a friend had sent from her Tennessee farm.

I had a hard time explaining to my mother, when she asked what my workdays now consisted of, that I spent a significant portion of my time pretending to be my cat online.

"But people *do* know that it's really you posting these things, right?" she asked.

"No, mom," I deadpanned. "People think that Homer is climbing onto the keyboard of my computer and typing these things himself."

It was a difficult thing to explain to a parent— although it felt perfectly natural and right to me. People would laugh at "Homer's" daily dispatches, and I was just as apt to laugh and sympathize with the comments and photos they posted themselves. Our regular readers would comment amusingly on my posts detailing Homer's doings, and they would also post pictures and updates about their own cats. I knew more cats on a first-name basis during this time than I ever had before. It might not be strictly accurate to say that I "knew" them—seeing as I'd never actually met them. But, then again, I knew them in the same way our readers knew Homer, through the stories their humans told, the concerns they shared, and the insights they offered when one or another of us would ask questions about preferred litter brands or appropriate diets for aging cats.

This all sounds about as "cat lady" as it gets—so I'll also add that, on occasion, our little community was able to do some real good. Every once in a while a shelter would write to me about an impossible-to-place blind cat and, inevitably, among Homer's community, we would find the perfect home for him. An acquaintance of mine living in Queens discovered two neglected cats in the basement of her apartment building. The building super had put them down there a year earlier, when they were only kittens, for the purpose of keeping the building rat-free. He'd barely thought about them since, and now my friend wanted to find a *real* home for them—one from which they could see the sunlight they'd never once experienced in their lives.

*Homer will never be able to see sunshine, but these two cats can...*my post about them began. Within only a few days, we had half a dozen firm offers of forever homes in the New York area alone. Geoffrey Jennings from Rainy Day Books in Kansas City—a passionate cat lover—offered a trove of autographed, first-edition, collectible books to go along with the cats to their new home. Five days later, all of us in Homer's community were rewarded with a picture of the two cats basking in the sunlight streaming through the bay window of a Brooklyn brownstone. The woman who adopted the cats named them Ellis, after Ellis Island, and Morgan, after the Morgan Library in Manhattan's East Thirties, because the cats had come to her with a library of their own.

We also chipped in small donations, in Homer's community, and were able to raise maybe a thousand dollars or so when natural disasters struck in various parts of the world—the kinds of tragedies that so often affected animals as well as humans, yet during which animals tended to be forgotten. My philosophy was that when you helped animals, you helped people, too—always remembering that the ASPCA, when they'd organized a rescue effort for pets in the wake of 9/11, had also helped people like me in the process. We collected food and other essentials and sent them to where they would do the most good.

Mostly, though, we simply enjoyed each other's company.

Not that everything was all positivity and sunshine. I soon learned that whereas novels are works of fiction, memoirs are true—and while (having written one of each) I'd always been aware of this technical distinction, what I hadn't thought about is that when readers don't like the "character" in your memoir, the person they actually dislike is you, yourself.

I heard from people who thought I was a heartless monster for having thought about my cats on 9/11, a day when so many human lives were lost; I heard from people who thought that I'd married a man who wasn't worthy of Homer; I heard from people who accused me of having adopted Homer twelve years earlier just so I'd someday be able to write a book about him. And I received one very long, very earnest email from an anonymous woman who was convinced that Homer had fallen ill in the months before my wedding because Laurence was slowly poisoning him with a household cleaning agent—in order to get rid of the competition, as it were, for my affections. Calling Laurence a "charismatic and sophisticated alpha male," she warned that he was likely to reveal his true, abusive nature at any moment, and advised me in the strongest possible terms to hire a private investigator to follow him—presumably so as to catch him in the act of being unfaithful.

"Follow me *where?*" Laurence seemed perplexed when I shared this email with him—albeit tickled at having been described as a *charismatic alpha male.* "You and I both work from home."

"I don't know," I replied. "But I'm going to start marking the levels on the Windex bottle—so don't get any ideas."

Poor Laurence! If only this letter-writer could have seen the grace with which—on the occasions when he joined me on one of my trips—Laurence accepted being referred to as "Mr. Cooper." (His last name is Lerman.)

But these were only a handful of negatives floating in an overwhelmingly positive sea. I had the daily joy of hearing every day from other animal lovers, from rescuers and people who were every bit as crazy about their own cats as I was about mine.

Homer's social-media community would continue to grow over the next couple of years. There was a big jump, after the paperback was published in 2010, when Homer's Facebook following expanded from two thousand to five thousand people within only a few months. But a lot of people seemed to "like" the page and then forget about it—so even when the numbers would appear to indicate otherwise, our core crew stayed more or less the same size. And, to tell the truth, at the time I liked it that way. Homer didn't have the kind of huge following that seemed likely to sell many books.

Then again, I'd never really seen Homer's Facebook page as a place to sell copies of *Homer's Odyssey.* It seemed probable that the only reason someone would follow the page was because they'd read the book already.

And, by then, Homer had gotten to be such a pro at posing for pictures, it seemed a shame to let his talents go to waste.

HOMER'S ONLINE COMMUNITY WAS always enjoyable, a place where I could post ongoing tales of Homer's amusing antics, a sounding board off of which I could bounce ideas for blog posts or new books as they came to me. But I'll always be truly grateful for the way our internet friends rallied around our family over the next two years, when first Vashti and then Scarlett fell to age-related illnesses.

Ultimately, this is Homer's story. I won't take you too far with me down the paths of confusion and sorrow that Laurence and I traveled during that time—paths well- trodden already by anyone who's loved an animal.

Suffice it to say that between the time when Vashti was diagnosed with chronic renal failure in late 2009, and the time when we lost her in August of 2010, there were many months during which she lived—a life that could only be sustained by a strenuous schedule of home treatment, which seemed overwhelming and impossible for me to undertake when her doctor first explained it. I was positive that I would fail Vashti in ways I couldn't imagine yet.

But, no matter how anxious or bewildered I felt, Homer's community was an unquenchable source of strength and insight.

By far the hardest part of Vashti's new care regimen was administering her every-other-day subcutaneous fluid injections, meant to help her body compensate for her failing kidneys. Vashti was a sweet girl who would tolerate just about anything we did to her, but it was easy to see how much she hated those injections—which weren't simply a shot, but a slow drip that had to be administered over the course of several long minutes. The subQ injections were the only thing Vashti really fought us on (and, bless her heart, she didn't fight hard—she merely struggled). Laurence had to hold her down while I inserted the tiny needle into the back of her neck, and sometimes she squirmed enough that the needle inadvertently hit a tender spot. Her tiny squeaks of pain whenever that happened left me ready to throw in the towel.

Many in Homer's community were old hands at the subQ routine. A few of them suggested a brilliant fix for us—heating the bag containing the solution in a pot of warm water until it came to Vashti's body temperature. This way, Vashti's experience would feel less like being immersed in a cold shower from inside her own body, and more like the pleasant relief of a warm bath.

Vashti and me, 2010

It was astonishing how immediate the difference was. After our first attempt with this new method, Vashti began to *like* her fluid injections. She would practically bounce with happiness by the time they were over, ready for a recently instituted ritual known as *Vashti's cuddle time.* "It's cuddle time!" Laurence or I would exclaim when the subQ was finished, and we'd climb into bed with Vashti eagerly following.

Alone in the bedroom with us—the door closed to keep the other cats out—she would enjoy one uninterrupted hour of exclusive time with both her humans, crawling first onto my chest and purring into my face for a few minutes as I stroked her back, before walking over to Laurence and doing the same with him. She'd spend the whole hour migrating back and forth between us while the warm fluids we'd just injected spread throughout her body, and when the sixty minutes were up she'd rejoin Scarlett and Homer, cheerful as ever.

It's hard watching an animal you love grow frailer— but Vashti was beautiful right up until the end. She did lose quite a bit of weight, but with her thick, lustrous coat of white fur it was nearly impossible to see, unless you knew her very well. And that fur never lost its silky luster. I have a picture of the two of us taken just days before the end, and in it Vashti literally glows, as if spot-lit from an unseen source.

The eternal feminine was what Laurence said of Vashti on her last day. It was something Lee Strasberg had said about Marilyn Monroe at her funeral, a way of describing the timeless, imperishable quality of her beauty—a beauty so overpowering, yet also so vulnerable, that it could reach right out and squeeze your heart until it ached.

Camille on her deathbed had nothing on our Vashti.

The paperback edition of *Homer's Odyssey* came out less than a month after we lost her. This time around, my publisher did spring for a small book tour—and, even though it wasn't near any of the four cities they'd originally planned to send me to, I insisted that the first stop be at Blind Cat Rescue & Sanctuary in North Carolina.

I'd seen pictures of many other blind cats since Homer's story was first published, but I still hadn't met many in the flesh. It was a moving experience to walk through Blind Cat Rescue, to enter room after room full of cats—cats who were young and old; white, gray, tabby, and calico; cats who were large and cats who were small; some who had long silky fur like Vashti's, and some who had practically no fur at all—but who all, nevertheless, looked like Homer. They raised questioning noses into the air just like Homer did, turned their heads from side to side like sonar dishes as they tried to "see" with their ears. And, even without eyes, their faces still managed to convey the joy they'd found in their life with each other, and with their human caregivers.

Vashti may only have been a support-ing player in *Homer's Odyssey*. But in our lives—our *real* lives—she'd always had one of three starring roles. Reading from Homer's book now, choosing a passage that included Vashti and Scarlett as well as Homer, and hav-ing just seen so many other "unadoptable" cats like Homer who'd nevertheless found happi-

Scarlett, 2011

ness in loving arms, was the first time I felt truly whole since Vashti had left us.

THERE WAS DECIDEDLY LESS *Homer* on Homer's Facebook page while all this was going on, but those core few who'd been with us from the beginning never complained or abandoned us. And they remained with us still in February of 2011, when Scarlett developed a sarcoma high on her left hind leg, the result of the rabies vaccination she'd gotten years earlier in Miami. (The specific formula that caused this sarcoma in some cats has been discontinued, by the way; you should always vaccinate your cats against rabies.)

In some ways, it was harder with Scarlett as her illness progressed than it had been with Vashti—not because it was so much worse or made her suffer more. But Scarlett had always been such a surly, feisty, irascible girl. She'd been born irritated with everybody and everything—even in her youth, she'd been the mean old lady who yells, *Get off my lawn, you kids!*

Our other cats bothered her. Laurence's mere existence—his insistence on living with us, despite her having made it perfectly clear that she'd prefer he left—was an ongoing annoyance. Guests in our home had obviously been sent by the devil himself, just so they could coo at her and make other friendly, insulting gestures until she was forced—in a state of high dudgeon—to *harrumph* her way into the seclusion of a bedroom. There were only two things in the world that Scarlett truly enjoyed— one of them was food, and the other was me. Anybody else, human or feline, was quickly reminded with a sharp *rowr!* and disciplinary smack of her paw to maintain their distance, leaving her to enjoy her wide berth of personal space in dignified peace.

Scarlett mellowed a great deal, however, during those last months—and I'll admit that it made me sad to see her become more accepting and tolerant as her health failed. I do think, though, that this change was partly because Homer was so considerate of her. He slept nearer to her than he'd ever dared before. But he no longer chased her, no longer tried to insert himself into her games of "chase the paper ball," no longer bothered her in any way. He stayed closer to Scarlett than he had in earlier years, but his closeness was far less intrusive.

We'd hoped that surgery to remove her tumor would solve the problem—and, when it didn't, we had difficult decisions to make.

There were many in Homer's community who advocated for removing Scarlett's leg altogether. But Scarlett was nearly seventeen, and arthritic, and she'd always been so poised and self-possessed that forcing her, at this point in her life, to adjust to getting around on only three legs seemed almost cruel. The same was true of chemotherapy. Others among our online friends had made different decisions for their own cats under similar circumstances. But everybody understood that Scarlett was Scarlett, and that there was no one-size-fits-all solution to these kinds of problems.

Scarlett had become so quiet and tractable by the time we knew it was over, in December of 2011, that it was almost as if she wasn't there anymore. She was the first cat I'd ever lived with, and there was a special pain in her loss. When I brought her to the vet for the last time, I couldn't even give my name to the receptionist without bursting into tears.

But Scarlett had one last gift for me. She'd been so silent and immobile in her carrier that I wasn't even sure she was still awake. But when the doctor very gently inserted the needle into her neck, Scarlett's eyes—which had been glazed and unfocused for the past day—quickly sharpened and narrowed. I knew by now that a needle so small, injected into the relatively insensitive scruff of her neck, wouldn't hurt her. But Scarlett still had enough of her personal dignity left to resent that a stranger had dared touch her at all. With her typical churlish *rowr!* of old, she reached up out of her cloth, blanket-lined carrier to take an annoyed swipe at the vet's hand. *Get off my lawn, you kids!*

It was so quintessentially *Scarlett* that I couldn't help but chuckle through my tears. *There's my surly girl!* For that brief moment, she wasn't the ailing, compliant Scarlett of the last few months. She was once again the crusty curmudgeon I'd loved so well for so long.

I would always say after that, in describing her final moments, that Scarlett had gotten to die as she'd lived— really, *really* pissed off.

HOMER TRULY GRIEVED WHEN we lost Scarlett, and Homer's community grieved with us. After about three days, when it became clear that she wasn't coming back, Homer seemed to age overnight. His customary run slowed to a walk, and his walk took on the stiff, wide-legged gait of an old man. He was no longer interested in chasing crumpled balls of paper across the living room, or in demanding bits of turkey from Laurence's sandwiches. Even a fresh sprinkling of home-grown catnip on the rug would leave him apathetic.

It was heartbreaking to see the transformation— made painfully ironic by the certainty I felt that Scarlett herself would have been perfectly content to be the last cat standing. As far as Scarlett was concerned, the best days of her life had been the earliest ones, when she was an only cat.

But Homer had always thought about his relationship with Scarlett very differently than Scarlett did. In Homer's mind, Scarlett was the (unwitting) supporting player in a thousand stalk-and-pounce adventure tales Homer liked to tell himself. She was his foil, his muse, his great nemesis, and he was never happier than when he'd finally succeeded in irritating her to the point that she would swat at him, nip at his neck, and then chase him down the hall before turning around to let him chase her back into the bedroom. While she hadn't been especially playful during her last months, she'd still been *there*—a comforting presence and warm scent, familiar for as long as he could remember, against which Homer could curl up and doze contentedly.

But it wasn't just the loss of Scarlett herself. Equally hard on Homer, I think, was the fact that he was now alone whenever Laurence and I were out. We had the luxury of spending far more time with Homer than most cat parents could with their own, simply because we worked from our apartment—but, still, we couldn't be home *all* the time. A trip to the vet, while unpleasant for all concerned (Homer's deep-seated hatred of the vet's office having only grown more intense with time), revealed that—physically, at least—he was in fine health.

What Homer needed more than anything was a new friend.

I thought that an older, more seasoned adult cat might make an ideal companion for Homer. Accordingly, I pulled first one owner-surrendered cat—and, when she and Homer didn't "click," another—from the euthanization lists at a New York open-intake shelter. My plan was to foster these cats and, if things worked out, to let them become "foster failures"—permanent members of our family.

There's always a period of adjustment when two adult cats get to know each other. Even in understanding this, however, things seemed particularly rough between Homer and first one, then the other, of the new cats we tried introducing him to. Poor Homer was utterly incapable of picking up on the visual body language of a wary cat. He had no way of seeing the arched back, the puffed tail, the backward steps of a cat who was unsure if Homer's approach was friendly or hostile. Scarlett and Vashti had known him since he was a kitten, and had grown accustomed to his seemingly odd ways. But to the cats we brought home now, Homer's eyeless black face must have appeared completely expressionless. He would approach them for a friendly, *how ya doin'?* mutual sniff, and was met with nothing but aggressive rebuffs.

Truth be told, I probably could have made it work with at least one of the cats if I'd really put the time in. But I didn't have the heart to subject Homer to any more stress after the loss of his two best friends. So I worked with a couple of the no-kill shelters I'd developed relationships with, and eventually we were able to find forever homes for both our fosters. (I still get pictures of them from their happy adoptive humans, and it always makes me smile.)

And that was how, early in 2012, we ended up adopting two little black kittens—litter-mates named Clayton and Fanny. Clayton had a damaged hind leg that we knew from the beginning would most likely have to come off sooner or later. (As it turned out—sooner.)

I'll tell their story in full later on. For now, it's enough to know that, even by kitten standards, Clayton and Fanny were ridiculously cheerful and high-spirited. There's probably nothing more irresistible than a kitten who adores you—and our kittens adored their new big brother immediately, right from the start. They were so playful, so eager to please, so ready to worship Homer in an abject, shameless way, that Homer would have had to be much more hard-hearted than he was to resist their charms. Homer couldn't see the goofy way Clayton would excitedly bunny-hop beside him on his three good legs, but I think Homer could sense it—and before long he was running, leaping, and chasing after toys, over the furniture and off the walls of our home, with all his old zest.

Ultimately, Homer recovered because he wasn't made for grief. It wasn't just that he was too innately happy—he was also too strong. Homer's strength was a force of nature, his will to live indomitable, as we would soon come to learn. All he needed in order to heal was a reminder that the world was still full of joy—that joy itself had been, and always would be, the very substance of his life.

I, of course, had known this about Homer all along. I'd written an entire book about it.

Playing the role of big brother was a new adventure for Homer. And new adventures were what Homer had always lived for.

Strong Like Bull

There is a time for many words,
and there is also a time for sleep.
-HOMER, *The Odyssey*

IT WAS A COLD, gray afternoon in early December, and I was
pulling our freshly cleaned winter bedding from the laundry bas-
ket, planning to swap it for the lighter sheets and blanket currently
dressing our bed. Homer and the kittens (who had, by now, grown
into full-fledged cats) were sitting in a semi-circle on the floor at
the foot of the bed. "Helping" me change the linens was always a
popular activity among our three. Homer would perform the vital
job of attacking each corner of the bed as the fitted sheet went over
it. Fanny pitched in by diving under the top sheet and creating a
lump I couldn't work around until I'd pushed her onto the floor.
And Clayton, not as good a jumper as the other two, would dig
in his front claws and haul himself up onto the bed—dragging
blanket and sheets halfway to the floor—and hop around after the

other two until I said, in an exasperated voice, "That's *enough!*" at which point he would flop down and look at me with deep reproach for having spoiled the game.

It was unquestionably a frustrating way to make the bed, but I couldn't help but smile now as I saw Homer's face turned up to mine in anticipation of one of our oldest and most cherished rituals. Homer was fifteen years old, and more apt than he'd used to be to choose naps over play. Where once he'd been the "poster kitty" for special-needs animals, he was now more of an elder statesman. His one gray whisker had become six, and the ebony sheen of his head was flecked with gray as well.

Fanny and Clayton had helped him recover the *joie de vivre* he'd lost after Scarlett's passing a year earlier. Still, I was bringing out the heavier blankets sooner than I normally would—usually I'd wait for the first snow—because I thought Homer might appreciate the additional warmth and softness a bit earlier this year.

I'd just gotten the old sheets off and dumped the new fitted sheet onto the middle of the bed, when I noticed that Homer, resting on his haunches, wobbled a bit before falling over to one side. He quickly righted himself, but fell over to the side again. Then he tried to stand, but his legs wouldn't support him. He went down in a small heap and curled all four paws beneath his body.

At first I wasn't even sure that I'd seen what I thought I saw. Maybe Homer was just lying down, and I had only imagined that something seemed "off." But then I saw how Homer struggled to hold his head up, like a kitten fighting to stay awake while falling asleep on his feet, and I knew that something was very wrong.

"Laurence!" In two long strides I was in the hallway and buried halfway to my chest in the hall closet as I struggled to free one of the cat carriers from its storage place. Clayton and Fanny had followed eagerly (*She opened the closet! Closets are awesome!*) and

I shooed them away impatiently. "*Laurence!*" I called again, and found that Laurence had already abandoned his home office next to our bedroom and was standing beside me.

"What happened?" he asked.

"There's something wrong with Homer. He just... fell over." I spoke calmly, not wanting to alarm Homer, who was always so attuned to the sound of my voice. "We have to get him to the animal hospital."

Laurence regarded me for a fraction of a second. It was only when I saw his face tighten with concern that I knew what my own looked like, despite the forced evenness of my tone. "Let's go," was all he said, and went to round up keys, coats, and cell phones.

Getting Homer into his carrier was usually an onerous task. Once upon a time, a trip in the carrier had meant a move to a new home and new territories for Homer to explore. But we'd lived here with Laurence for just over seven years now—nearly half of Homer's life. These days, the carrier meant only one thing: the vet.

There was nothing in the world Homer loathed and feared as much as the vet's office. He'd never exactly been a *good* patient, but the problem had gotten exponentially worse over the years. The last time we'd gone, in January, I'd had to cradle Homer in my arms in order for the vet to get close enough to draw a blood sample. When the needle went in, Homer had panicked and bitten my hand so hard that I'd had to go the emergency room later for a tetanus shot. He'd seemed immediately remorseful upon hearing my yelp of pain, struggling to get his front paws onto my shoulder so he could nuzzle my neck, the way he had that very first day we'd met, all those years ago. When the vet had tried to approach him again, he'd hissed at her wildly over my shoulder, like a thing possessed. *Leave me alone!* he seemed to say. *Look what you made me do to my human!*

We hadn't been back since.

Homer didn't struggle at all now. He was still breathing, and he appeared to be awake. But whether he was on the floor or in his carrier seemed to be a matter of equal indifference to him.

Seeing his utter lack of resistance made the knots in my stomach tighten. I held him for a moment, pressing my cheek to the top of his head before gently lowering him in. "You're going to be fine," I assured him in a soft voice. "You'll be just fine."

It was the lunch hour—always a difficult time to catch a cab in front of our Midtown apartment—so Laurence walked a couple of blocks up while I huddled Homer in his carrier as close under my coat as I could, trying to keep him warm. With my cell phone cradled between my shoulder and my ear, I let the receptionist at the vet's office know that Homer and I were on our way in with an emergency. As I hung up, I saw the blessed sight of Laurence in the back of a cab pulling up to us.

Homer didn't budge or call out once during the entire ten-minute ride—also very unlike him—and I found myself unable to stop unzipping the top of the carrier just far enough to slip my hand in, to stroke Homer's head and side and make sure he was still breathing. The traffic on First Avenue was too heavy for our cabbie to cross, forcing him to drop us across the street from the animal hospital's entrance. I left Laurence to pay him and, like the true New Yorker I'd long-since become, darted into the street against the light, breaking into a run so none of the oncoming cars would have to slow to avoid me. I was slightly out of breath by the time I reached the receptionist's desk and placed Homer in his carrier on top of it.

Reina, the woman behind the desk, knew me well. I'd been there at least once a month during the two years when Vashti and Scarlett were sick, and more recently when Clayton had to have his hind leg removed. Laurence and I liked to say that we'd probably financed a Cooper-Lerman Memorial Wing of the animal hospital, given our outrageous expenses there over the past few years. It was a joke, of course, but I don't think I'd ever felt less like laughing than I did in that moment, finding myself yet again in that familiar waiting room.

"What happened?" Reina asked, making sympathetic clucking sounds at Homer through the mesh sides of the carrier.

"I don't know. He just kind of fell over," I told her.

Reina pressed a button on her phone that summoned a vet tech through the swinging door that led to the exam rooms in the back. She took the carrier from Reina but turned to stop me when I tried to follow. "You'll have to wait out here," she said kindly, but firmly.

"But I have to go with him." My voice was calm. *Just two reasonable people having a reasonable disagreement.* "He's blind, and he's terrified of the vet's office. I don't think you'll be able to handle him without me."

She peered at Homer, silent and stone-still in his carrier. He'd always been a little guy, but now he looked positively frail. "I think we'll manage." She smiled reassuringly. "We have to bring him to the tech area for tests," she explained, "and there are other animals back there. That's why we need you to wait out here."

I turned to Reina, who was also our pet-sitter when we traveled and knew Homer better than anyone else at the clinic, hoping for a reprieve. "He'll be fine, *mami.*" Behind her, the vet tech had already disappeared with Homer back through the swinging door. "He's so out of it, he probably won't even know what's going on."

I took the seat Laurence had saved for me in the cozy, wood-paneled waiting area—made welcoming with posters of puppies and kittens, flyers for pet-sitters, and copies of *Best Friends* magazine—and tried to imagine what went on when a nearly unconscious cat was brought into a veterinary emergency room. My sole knowledge of what happened when someone was rushed unconscious to the hospital came from television and movies. Would they plop Homer onto a gurney and wheel him speedily into another room while a doctor called for CCs of this and tests for that? Would nurses cluster around trying to get blood pressure and pulse readings? I was heartsick, miserable at the thought of Homer—tiny Homer, weakened and terrified—being subjected to unknown probes and prods and lord-only-knew-what-else without me there to comfort him.

But, as it turned out, I was luckier than I realized. I wouldn't have to wonder for long.

The tech area, where Homer had been taken, was all the way in the back of the building, and the waiting area was in the front. Separating them was a long corridor with exam rooms branching off from it. We were probably a good hundred feet away from Homer, with two closed doors (one at either end of the corridor) between us. Nevertheless, within a few minutes I heard what was going on.

Everybody heard what was going on.

Over the years, I've probably heard the full range of sounds that the average housecat is capable of making—the meows, burbles, and coos; the purring and deep-throated whines; the shrill, unforgettable screams of a cat who's enraged or terrified. Homer himself had always had an especially rich vocal repertoire, with a series of highly distinct mews, yips, and growls meant to indicate things like, *I can't find you; I'm hungry; I'm coming over to be petted now;* and *This is irritating me.*

What I heard now wasn't any of those. It hardly even sounded like noises a cat should be capable of making—and, at first, I didn't think it *was* a cat. I didn't even think that the sound came from any natural source. For a second, I thought that maybe a nearby construction worker had started up a chainsaw. But, after the briefest of pauses for breath, it became clear that these were animal noises—the sound of some enraged wild beast fending off hunters or defending its territory. The vicious, furious snarls rose in volume to fill the entire waiting room, so deep now, so sustained, so impossibly loud, that they could only be described as roars.

It was lunchtime, the busiest time of day at the animal clinic, and the waiting room was packed. There were huge dogs and tiny ones at the ends of leashes, cats and rabbits in carriers, two cages containing a parrot and a parakeet. Every animal was accompanied by a human, and it was something of a miracle that Laurence had managed to score us two seats at all.

As the roars from the back of the hospital continued and grew in both volume and anger, the comfortable hum of conversation and scuffling animals in the waiting room fell silent. Reina, from her station behind the receptionist's desk, put the call she was taking on hold and turned to stare in open-mouthed wonder at the door leading to the back. For a breathless moment, the entire animal hospital was dead silent except for the enraged clamor rising from the back. Then a hushed murmuring rose in the waiting room, as if everybody was instinctively wary of elevating their voices above a whisper. *What the...? What's going on back there? What* is *that?* One woman, in an undertone, said something that ended with...*a panther?* The man she was with muttered darkly about the kind of idiot who thought it was okay to keep exotic pets in a New York apartment.

Two large dogs had begun to whimper and cringed behind the legs of their owners, while a smaller dog issued a low rumble, the hackles raised on the back of his neck. From the dark recesses of carriers, I heard hisses and growls. The parakeet twittered and fluttered frantically around his cage. I thought of my younger sister, who'd always shrieked so loudly and continuously when receiving childhood shots that every other kid in the pediatrician's waiting room would break into terrified sobs.

"What do you think it is?" Laurence whispered.

I threw him a wry, sideways look.

"You think that's *Homer?*" Laurence appeared dubious. But then his glance took in my face, which felt so hot that I knew it had to be fiery red. His expression changed from incredulity to awe. "Damn," he muttered.

I was already standing when the door to the back swung open, and I nearly walked right into the vet tech who'd initially brought Homer to the back of the hospital. She'd been so calm and confident when we'd first come in, but now she was profoundly flustered. Her face looked as red as mine had felt a moment ago, and I could see that her hands were trembling. "They need you back there," she blurted. Pointing down the hallway, she added, "The last exam room on the left." Once she'd made sure I was going the right way, she ducked into a small side room, quickly closing the door behind her.

I felt a bit like a character in a scary movie as I headed in the direction the vet tech had indicated—some not-very-bright girl inexplicably walking toward the room containing the terrifying monster, rather than away from it. I'd known that the sounds I'd heard in the waiting room would only grow louder as I approached their source, but it was still unnerving to hear *how much* louder they became.

The tableau that greeted me when I reached Homer's exam room might have been comical under different circumstances. Standing in a semicircle—facing the high metal exam table bolted to the wall, but at a judicious distance from it—were three women.

One was the doctor, who must have been new to the practice, because I'd never seen her before. The other two were clearly assistants. They'd donned long, thickly padded gloves that stretched from the tips of their fingers all the way up to their shoulders, like the ones that falconers wear. They'd also knotted bandanas behind their ears and pulled them up protectively over their faces. Their foreheads above the bandanas were a vivid pink and beaded with sweat. Their bodies were poised with a tense wariness, leaning slightly forward at the shoulders while their feet were half-turned in the opposite direction, ready to carry them back to a safer distance if the need arose.

Seeing Homer—all four pounds of him, crouched defensively on the exam table—took me back instantly, all the way to that summer night more than twelve years earlier, when a Homer I hadn't recognized had chased a large male intruder right out of our Miami apartment. If he'd looked helpless and fragile a half-hour ago, when I'd first brought him in to the clinic, he now more closely resembled the panther the woman in the waiting room had thought she'd heard. The hind part of his body was elevated and his chest was lowered until it almost touched the table beneath him. His head was raised with his mouth wide open, lips pulled back in a cruel rictus that bared all his teeth. His head and ears moved evenly from side to side as he listened for a cue as to where the next assault might come from, one paw raised with claws at full extension, ready to lash out as soon as someone came within striking distance.

One of the assistants was holding a yellowish hand towel in front of her, the way a lion tamer might hold a chair between himself and the roaring lion before him. As I entered, the assistant—still maintaining a safe distance between herself and Homer—gingerly tossed it over his head. Homer immediately erupted into a fresh round of anguished, deafening roars, thrashing angrily as his claws attempted to escape the towel and find his tormentors.

I knew that putting a towel over the head of a distressed cat was standard procedure, that it usually *calmed* them, and that the hot bolt of rage that stabbed from my chest to my belly was therefore unwarranted. Everybody in that room wanted only to help Homer. Still, it took a wrenching effort of will to make my voice sound as serene as it needed to, for Homer's sake.

"Okay, so Homer is blind." I said *Homer* in the gentle, sing-song cadence I used at home when I was particularly happy with him. The wild thrashing beneath the towel stilled. "Putting a cloth over his head isn't going to quiet him the way it does other cats. You're just making him more upset."

The assistant who'd thrown the towel now leaned forward and, grabbing the corner closest to her and farthest from Homer's claws, quickly pulled it off while simultaneously taking a large step back. The Homer thus revealed, puffed up to several times his normal size, bore little resemblance to the Homer I knew. Nevertheless, his ears had pricked up and turned toward my voice. Once freed from the towel, his nose followed, rising inquisitively in an attempt to discern whether there was a familiar scent to match the familiar cadence.

"You're a good boy, Homer." I approached him slowly, my hands raised in front of me in an instinctive gesture of non-threatening compliance that was, of course, wasted on a blind cat. Cautiously, I put one hand directly beneath his nose.

Homer immediately pressed his whole face into my cupped palm, and I used the other hand to rub gently behind his ears. As frightening as it had been to see Homer in his rage, my heart nearly broke now to see him morph back into his normal self—just a scared little cat, terrified out of his wits at being separated from the human he trusted.

"You're a good boy, Homer, a good, good boy," I repeated soothingly, and Homer's fur sank as his entire body seemed to relax.

If I'd levitated into the air right in front of them, the vet and her assistants couldn't have appeared more gobsmacked as Homer transformed from snarling beast to docile housecat in my hands. "I'm sorry," the vet said. "With the way he was brought in, we didn't know he'd put up such a fight."

I told you so! I told you so! a voice in my brain shrieked. But I only laughed ruefully and said, "I understand. It *is* hard to believe that such a little guy can make such a big ruckus."

"He's so *teeny!*" one of the assistants exclaimed almost indignantly, as if she'd been trying to restrain herself but couldn't hold it in any longer—couldn't quite fathom how one small cat, and a sick one at that, had been able to cause three grown women who handled animals *for a living* to fear legitimately for their physical safety.

"Maybe you should spend a few minutes alone with him," the vet said now. "It looks like we'll have to sedate him before we can examine him. That might go easier if he's a little calmer before I try to inject him."

"That's a good idea," I said. "Is it okay if I sit on the floor?"

At her nod, I sat down cross-legged about a foot from the exam table. "Come here, Homer-Bear," I said, and Homer leapt a touch awkwardly from the table to the ground. In the crouched, creeping way of an animal that suspects it's being hunted, he made his way over to where I sat and crawled into my lap. The three women, still shaking their heads in amazement, filed silently out of the room.

Homer and I sat there for long minutes as I continued to stroke him. He didn't purr, and he didn't fall asleep, but he did fall into a calm, quiet reverie. *My poor boy,* I thought. *My poor, poor boy.* At this point, I felt well beyond guilty and heartily sorry that I'd brought Homer in at all, knowing how very traumatic the vet always was for him—although what choice had I had? Eventually, the vet returned and knelt over us just long enough to jab a needle into the back of Homer's neck. Homer instantly hissed and reared up, trying to catch her with his front claws. But the sedative kicked in pretty quickly, and Homer fell unconscious back into my lap.

"We can take it from here," the vet said, lifting Homer and bundling him back into his carrier. "We'll draw blood and run some tests. I'll let you know when he's ready to leave."

Laurence and I had to wait another half hour before we were able to bring a still-sedated Homer back home. I was given some instructions on how to care for him and things to watch for until the sedative wore off. "Do you know what caused him to fall over like that this afternoon?" I asked. After all the drama of the preceding hour, the thing that had brought us there in the first place seemed almost like an afterthought, like something that had happened years ago to somebody else.

"We'll know more when the bloodwork comes back tomorrow," the vet told me. "We'll call you as soon as we have it. The important thing now is for him to get some rest."

HOMER SLEPT FOR THE rest of the afternoon. He didn't stir into consciousness again until early evening, when he woke just long enough to eat his dinner before staggering back into the bedroom and collapsing in the little nest I'd made for him on the floor from old t-shirts and sweaters.

I moved his litter-box into our bedroom and kept him in there with us overnight, away from the curious noses of Clayton and Fanny, who couldn't figure out why their big brother smelled so different (like the vet's office, although they didn't know it), and why he didn't wake and acknowledge them, even when they touched his head and face with tentative little paws. At some point in the middle of the night, Homer made an unsuccessful attempt to jump onto the bed but fell over backwards, the sedative having still not worn off entirely. I didn't want him on the bed—which, being a king-size, was rather high off the ground—because I wasn't sure he'd be able to jump off without hurting himself if he needed his litter-box. But I also didn't want him to have to sleep by himself. I ended up moving my pillows and a blanket down to the floor, so I could curl up next to him.

The next morning, Homer was almost miraculously back to his old self. He ate a big breakfast and greeted Clayton and Fanny in his usual imperious way. A couple of hours later we were playing one of his favorite games, wherein I would wriggle my finger under the

Homer, December 2012

bed covers and Homer (who could once again get on and off the bed just fine) would pounce on them. I was delighted to see him cocking his head to one side in familiar fashion as he listened for the slight noises that would pinpoint where, exactly, my fingers were.

He was still doing well enough when noon came around that Laurence and I went out to grab a quick lunch at a sandwich place next to our apartment building. We'd just placed our orders when my cell phone rang with a call from the animal hospital. The vet who called wasn't the one who had seen Homer yesterday, but she assured me that she'd thoroughly read both Homer's test results and his medical file.

"How's he doing today?" she asked.

"He seems okay, actually." I'd risen and was walking through the restaurant, so we could continue the call outside where I wouldn't disturb the diners around me. "He was even playing this morning."

She sounded surprised. "He was *playing*?"

I think I mistook her surprise for reproach—as if she were implying that I was a dangerous lunatic for running an invalid cat like Homer around—and I quickly backtracked. "It wasn't *strenuous* play. He was in a playful mood, is what I meant."

"No, that's good!" She seemed to file this tidbit away for future reference before continuing. "So I've looked over the bloodwork and Homer's file, and I wanted to go over the results with you."

She started with the numbers that fell within the normal range and therefore looked good, and that was the shortest part of our conversation. The problem, it quickly became clear, was Homer's liver. I didn't have to understand all the ins and outs or medical jargon to know immediately how serious the problem was. Doing some rapid calculations, I realized that Homer's liver values (the enzymes that were supposed to be found in the liver itself, not in his bloodstream) were about fifteen hundred percent higher than what was normal in a cat. *Fifteen hundred percent!* "If his fur wasn't so black, you'd probably have noticed a while ago that his ears are yellow, and how jaundiced he is," the vet told me, and I cursed myself for having been so stupid—so unforgivably stupid and unobservant. "I sounded surprised when you said Homer was playing this morning, because frankly a cat with numbers like these shouldn't even be able to walk." She didn't say it aloud, but I knew what she was thinking: *He shouldn't even be alive.*

My mind instantly rejected that thought. Numbers or no numbers, anybody with two eyes in their head could see that Homer was still *Homer.* He ate, he played, he cuddled in my lap. Maybe on paper he shouldn't be alive, but in the real world he was still walking around the same as ever—and where there was life, there was hope. So I took a deep breath to steady myself and asked, "Where do we go from here?"

"I'd like you to bring Homer in this afternoon," the vet said, "and plan on leaving him here for a few days— maybe a week." She launched into her recommended course of treatment, an aggressive one that would involve hooking Homer up round-the-clock to various drips and medications, which would drain harmful fluids out and introduce healthier ones in, and give his liver a fighting chance to recover.

I didn't even know I'd started to cry until I became aware of a pain on my cheeks, and realized that the icy December wind had frozen the tears to my face. *My god,* was all I could think. *My god, how can I do this to him? How can I bring him back to that place and leave him there all alone?*

"Let me talk to the doctor who saw Homer yesterday," the vet concluded. "I'll call you back so we can make a plan."

Laurence was waiting at our table when I re-entered the restaurant, and I saw that our food had arrived in my absence. I couldn't touch mine, however, and as I relayed to Laurence the substance of my conversation with the vet, my tears began to flow in earnest. He reached across the table to cover my hand with his and tried to say something comforting. I suddenly became aware that we were in a very public place, and that the other patrons closest to us were beginning to take an interest in our table. "I'm sorry," I said, and my voice sounded like I was choking. "I have to go back outside. People will think you're breaking up with me." I got up and left him for a second time, crouching once I'd reached the sidewalk again and putting my head between my legs as I tried to pull myself together.

I was still outside, grateful for the cold air I inhaled in greedy gulps in the hopes it would clear my thoughts, when the vet called back. "I spoke with the doctor who saw Homer yesterday," she told me. "We talked a bit and..." She hesitated, as if searching for the right words. "We're not sure that Homer would benefit from a hospital environment."

For a moment, I was hopeful. "You mean you think I can treat him at home?"

Her voice softened. "Look, the doctor you saw yesterday told me what happened. We can't get near Homer without sedating him, and we can't keep a cat fully sedated for days at a time. And we can't sedate a cat at *all* with bloodwork like Homer's. If we'd known how bad his numbers were, we wouldn't have sedated him yesterday."

"So you're saying you can't treat him without sedating him, but you can't sedate him until you've been able to treat him."

"That's about it," the vet agreed. "The thing is, even the really mean cats, when they have numbers like these, are usually so sick and weak that we can do whatever we need to with them. I don't know how much longer Homer's strength can last—it's a miracle that it's lasted this long— but as long as it does, there's really nothing to be gained by you bringing him back here."

She was, as I would later recount at innumerable shelter readings whenever I told this story, saying to me in the nicest possible way, *Please don't ever bring your demon cat back to our animal hospital again.* I couldn't argue. I was no more anxious to bring Homer back than they were to have him.

"Is there anything I can do for him by myself?"

"I'm going to write you a couple of prescriptions," she said. "Some medication to support his liver and other functions. There's a pharmacy uptown that can compound it with something yummy-tasting like chicken or tuna. That way you can just squirt it into his mouth or mix it with his food, instead of trying to pill him. It's a two-week course of treatment."

My voice cracked when I spoke again, dreading the answer even before I asked the question. "What do we do for him when the two weeks are up?"

"I'm sorry," she said, and the sorrow in her voice was genuine. "But Homer's numbers are incompatible with life."

It was an awful phrase, *incompatible with life*—at once so brutal yet efficiently descriptive that it told the whole story. So it seemed almost superfluous when she went on to add:

"I don't think he has more than two weeks left."

As a kindness to my fellow sensitive readers (and I'm assuming that applies to most of you reading this), I'll risk ruining the suspense and tell you up front that we did *not* lose Homer within the next two weeks. Nor did we lose him within four weeks, or even four months. Homer, as it turned out, had more fight left in him than even those of us who knew him best (and had seen him at his worst) thought he was capable of. In the end, he would stay with us for the better part of the next year.

But, at the time, we still had to go through it all and make our decisions without knowing outcomes. Looking back now, I realize that I didn't really have any decisions to make. Homer had made them already. All I could do was let things take whatever course they were going to take. But I didn't know this then—or perhaps it's more honest to say that it was a knowledge I resisted.

It was hard to believe that Homer's condition could really be as dire as the vet had said. I scanned his ears anxiously when Laurence and I got home from the restaurant, and indeed, when I looked at them closely, the insides had a definite yellow cast beneath the black of his fur. But Homer quickly grew impatient with his ear exam. He was far more interested in the bag I'd brought home containing my uneaten sandwich. After downing a generous helping of sliced turkey—which pretty much depleted my sandwich entirely, and it was astonishing to watch Homer put away a quantity of food that would have more than filled *me* up—Homer trotted over to his bed on the desk beside my computer, waiting patiently for me to sit down after lunch as I usually did, and spend the afternoon typing away with him by my side. It was as if yesterday hadn't happened.

I spent the next two weeks on a sort of doomsday watch. Every time Homer ate a meal with gusto (which was pretty much every meal), I counted it as a triumph. Every time I watched him chase a crinkle ball around, every time he cuddled up to have me spoon him on the couch, I thought, *Is this it? Is this the last time?* Every time he was slower to awaken from a nap than I thought he should be, I wondered if he was going to wake up at all.

I watched and I wondered—and I agonized. What was I to do for him? When Vashti had been diagnosed with chronic renal failure (and hyperthyroidism, and high blood pressure, and anemia), I'd forced pills down her throat once a day, and given her shots twice a day, and administered subcutaneous fluid injections every other day. I'd taken her to the vet for monthly check-ups and twice she'd had to stay there overnight. Scarlett had had surgery for her cancer, and I'd had to give her insulin shots twice a day for her diabetes. Certainly none of it could be described as *fun*— and the two of them had struggled and fled and clawed and even hissed on occasion enough for me to know how much they disliked all the poking and prodding and pilling—but all that had been a few unpleasant minutes out of our days, which the two of them seemed to forget completely as soon as it was over. And the reward for those unpleasant few minutes was the additional time we had together that we wouldn't have had otherwise.

But Homer wasn't like Vashti and Scarlett. For the past few years, he wouldn't even let me trim his claws anymore. I had known even before Homer got sick—back when I was going through everything I went through with my two girls—that I wouldn't be able to do the same for him. Regular vet visits would be difficult enough, probably even impossible. As much as Homer loved and trusted me, I knew he'd never let me pill him regularly, or stick needles in him. The best-case scenario was that I'd win those battles (maybe!) but end up injured and bloodied for my efforts, and Homer would come to fear my scent and the sound of my voice as much as he'd ever feared the vet's office. Homer would never understand why I was doing all these terrible things to him. What would be the point of extending his life only to rob him of all the security and love and trust he'd built that life on?

There would be no point, I had assured myself, back when Homer was healthy and these were only abstract thoughts.

But now the abstract had become concrete, and the sand beneath my feet had shifted. I couldn't just do nothing, could I? I mean, maybe I couldn't do *anything*—but I certainly couldn't do *nothing.* The collective wisdom of Homer's Facebook community recommended milk thistle, which I began liberally sprinkling into his drinking water. Perhaps it helped. But it certainly didn't seem like the kind of heroic measures I should be taking on his behalf. How could a few drops of milk thistle be sufficient when I was willing to do anything—literally, *anything*—that could be done for Homer, if only he would let me help him?

I remember one day when it was especially bad with me, when the certainty that I was losing Homer and could do nothing to stop it was the only certainty I had in the world, and it sat in my chest so heavily I could hardly breathe. I was at my computer, and Homer was sitting on his haunches on the desk next to me, leaning the entire weight of his body heavily against my left shoulder, as he did when he sensed that I needed comfort. I went to his Facebook page and, unlike my usual habit of posting funny pictures and amusing little stories, typed a single sentence. *How will I live without this cat?* I quickly deleted it, embarrassed at having posted such a stark (and melodramatic) cry of pain on a Facebook page for anybody to see. But it had been seen already, and my phone rang a few minutes later.

Some months earlier, out on the "cat circuit," I'd struck up a friendship with Jackson Galaxy—Animal Planet's famous and infamous "Cat Daddy"—and, as it turned out, he was every bit as compassionate in real life as one would expect from his show. He'd called now to see how Homer and I were doing, and I laid out my dilemma for him, sparing no details in describing Homer's recent visit to the animal hospital. I concluded by asking him

Homer & Jackson Galaxy, 2012

the same question I'd been asking myself non-stop for days: Didn't

I have to do something more for Homer—try some new doctor, some kind of medical treatment, *something* more than what I was doing?

Jackson listened until I'd talked myself out. "Homer is sending you a very clear message," he said when I'd finished. "And that message is *DO. NOT. WANT. I do not want this!* It's not fair to ignore a cat when he's talking to you that loudly and clearly."

"But how can I just do *nothing* for him?"

"Treating Homer with respect and dignity isn't nothing," Jackson told me. "Seeing him through this last phase of his life—however long that might be—with mindfulness and love isn't nothing." He paused for a moment, as if collecting his thoughts. "You have to be selfless now," he finally said. "You made an unspoken deal with Homer the day you adopted him. In loving him, you promised you'd always take care of him. Taking care of someone means putting them before you. And that means you, in this moment, don't matter. Your sadness doesn't matter. You'll have plenty of time for that when he leaves. In this moment, you're a parent with only one job. You have to listen to Homer, because the only promise to keep is not to wait until it's his worst day. Let him leave knowing love, not fear, not pain, not the flipside of love. Do you really want, *now*, to rob him of all that love and confidence he's had in such abundance his whole life?"

"No." My voice was husky. "No, I really don't."

"Just because doctors *can* do something doesn't mean they should. Just because you did certain things for your other cats doesn't mean you should do them for *this* cat. Every cat is different. You should follow Homer's lead."

"But Homer doesn't understand the choice he's making. He doesn't know what I know." I truly did want to let it go, to accept the reality of what was happening and make my peace with it. But the struggle had been too hard for me to give it up all at once.

"He knows what *he* knows. Maybe that's enough," Jackson concluded. "And Homer might end up surprising you. Cats usually do."

JACKSON'S WORDS PROVED TO be prophetic. Days became weeks became months, and still Homer was with us. Still the same Homer more or less, although he did eventually slow a bit, like a clock just beginning to wind down.

The worst thing a cat can do for his liver is to stop eating—but, paradoxically, cats with liver disease are usually reluctant eaters at best. The challenge is to keep them eating, at least enough to give their liver something to do other than eat itself.

Homer, however, had always been a cat who defied expectations, and he ate voraciously. To say that Homer became a non-stop eating machine would be an understatement—and trying to describe what it was like to watch a four-pound cat eat his body weight every day is one of the rare times when words have failed me. It started with the medication the vet had prescribed, which apparently was every bit as yummy as promised when mixed with his regular food. When the two weeks' worth of medication ran out, I made it my mission to keep the food party going. At first I started out with some kitten-hood favorites, long- since abandoned on health grounds—although my new philosophy was, *As long as he's eating and he's happy.* Kitten Chow once again became a permanent fixture in our cupboard, and Homer attacked it with so much zeal that it almost seemed as if eating the food he'd eaten when he was younger made him feel like a young cat again. Gooey cans of Friskie's and Fancy Feast also found their way into Homer's food bowl.

But it was Laurence who really rose to the occasion. What was, for me, a medical imperative became a genuine source of pleasure for Laurence, and finding new and exciting foods to tempt Homer with was his passion. That Homer was eating at all was less surprising than *how much* he was eating, consuming more than enough food in the typical day to satisfy a grown man.

Homer and Laurence, 2013

Laurence brought Homer imported European canned tunas, sliced turkey by the pound, hamburgers, prime rib, shredded roast beef, pork-fried rice, spare ribs, pizza cheese, Gerber's baby food, and lobster dipped in butter. (The only thing Homer was particular about was his lobster—which was heaven on earth when dipped in butter, but unworthy of his interest when it was not.) He brought home salmon salad and whitefish salad from our favorite bagel place, and a stinky cheese from Murray's in the West Village that was so very stinky—even when stowed in the refrigerator—we'd had to ditch it a day later, even though the aroma had Homer clawing at the refrigerator door as if his very life depended on getting in.

Laurence's imagination ranged from the high to the low, and he also brought home mysterious "potted meats" found in fifty-cent cans at our local bodega, which Homer gobbled down as enthusiastically as if it were caviar (which Homer also grew to love during that final year). Cans of Vienna Sausages—again from our bodega—mashed with a fork and served *au jus* were a particular treat. Chinese chicken on the bone from the take-out place across the street was a big hit, although not nearly as tempting as a fried chicken breast from Popeye's, the smell of which drove Homer absolutely wild with delight. Homer could polish off an entire Popeye's breast in the space of half an hour, although perhaps Homer's greatest culinary accomplishment was the time he finished an entire mutton chop—literally bigger than he was!—that Laurence brought home from the legendary Keen's Steakhouse. (In fairness, I should add that it did take him two days to eat his way through the whole thing.) The image of little Homer, sitting in front of that giant mutton chop like a tiny Henry VIII about to dig into a palace banquet, is one I'll always be grateful to have in my memory.

Perhaps the only truly perplexing food that Homer developed a taste for was carrot cake. I'd brought home a slice without frosting from a health-food place, saving it as an after-dinner treat for myself. But a couple of hours later I found Homer on the kitchen counter, clawing off the plastic it was wrapped in and gobbling the cake down greedily. I was on the verge of stopping him—carrot cake striking me as an odd and potentially unhealthy choice for a cat. But then I thought, *why not?* and carried the rest to his bowl, for him to finish at his leisure.

It was clear to us that Homer was waging a tremendous battle, one that required an almost incomprehensible amount of fuel to keep it going. It seems to me now, looking back, that forgoing aggressive medical care turned out to be the right decision, if only because Homer would have fought it, and me, every step of the way. He almost certainly couldn't have battled on two fronts with nearly as much success as he battled now on just the one.

But even with all his strength—and I'll admit that I was a bit awed, this late in Homer's life, to realize fully just how tremendous that strength actually was—the battle was taking its toll. He napped far more than he used to, and lost weight until he was barely more than skin and bones. Running my hand down his back, I could feel every vertebra in his spine. His coat, once so lustrous and sleek, began to look oily. But as long as Homer still played and ate, as long as he still cuddled and purred and chased Fanny and Clayton around, I told myself that I would let him fight for his life on his own terms, without taking anything away from him.

Our bedroom became Homer's bedroom, and he slept with me every night. Whether because he was confused, or too tired to make the effort of jumping from the bed and walking to his litter-box (which I'd moved permanently into our bedroom), the bed became his nighttime litter-box during those last few months. Honesty compels me to add that those nighttime poops were...something—although who among us hasn't cleaned up that and worse while caring for an ailing cat? And, given both the size and nature of Homer's new daily diet, what else could be expected?

Laurence moved temporarily into the guest bedroom, and I put a rubber sheet over our mattress. Stripping off all the sheets and blankets, I made a little nest for Homer from some of my old t-shirts and sweaters. As for myself, I slept wrapped up, cocoon-style, in a comforter. Homer and I were still able to cuddle, and it made clean-ups much easier.

I realize that, in the retelling, this sounds like an odd and cumbersome way to live—although it's amazing how quickly the unusual becomes routine when it's the landscape of your everyday life. I never thought of it as an imposition at all. I *wanted* to be there for all this—not just the playtimes and the cuddling, but the late-night cleanings and nursing Homer through bouts of upset stomach and every last messy, inconvenient bit of it. Once upon a time, I had saved Homer's life. And then, years later, he had saved mine. I can honestly say that I never loved Homer more than any of the other animals I've been lucky enough to live with. But Homer and I were bound to each other in a way that was nothing like anything I had experienced before—and I knew that I would never have anything in my life quite like this again. I couldn't have felt more tied to Homer if he'd literally been flesh of my flesh, bone of my bone.

When spring came, I resumed my schedule of shelter readings and fundraising appearances. Because I worked from home and spent, in the typical day, twenty-one hours or more within ten feet of Homer, it should have been easier to leave him once or twice a month for an afternoon trip upstate or a twenty-four-hour overnight to speak at a shelter farther away. Paradoxically, though, the more time I spent with Homer, the harder it was to go away from him. Still, talking about him at these events was a source of deep, deep pleasure.

People always asked about Homer during the Q&A sessions after I'd finished reading. Was he still alive? Was he in good health? I would tell the story of that last visit to the vet's office, how Homer—tiny Homer, sick as he was!— had overpowered the staff and thrown the entire animal hospital into disarray. I told them of the dire predictions that Homer wouldn't last out the month, wouldn't live to see the New Year. But here it was, the following summer, and Homer was still with us! A little slower, perhaps, and a little skinnier, but eating like a champ and enjoying his life. People would shake their heads in astonishment.

How was such a thing possible? How could such a little cat have so much fight in him? It became a standard part of these talks, of telling this story, for me to clench my right hand into a fist and strike the left side of my chest—just over my heart. In my best approximation of a Russian accent, I would proudly declare:

"Because my cat is strong like bull."

HOMER *WAS* STRONG LIKE a bull—and he'd fought hard and far longer than any bull in a ring ever had. But it was a fight we'd always known couldn't go on forever.

The end came one late-August afternoon, nearly four years to the day since *Homer's Odyssey* had first been published. Laurence and I had gone out to run a few errands. When I walked back in through our front door, the first thing I saw was Homer hanging from the side of the couch, his front legs splayed out to full extension as he dangled from two claws—one in each front paw—that had become snagged in the fabric as he'd tried to pull himself up. Too exhausted to try very hard to free himself, he simply dangled, waiting mutely for me to find him and help.

I'd noticed that Homer had slowed down even more in the past few days, that he'd gone from being tired to being *tired*, not stirring from his spot on the couch unless it was time for him to eat or follow me into the bedroom for the night. I'd also noticed that Clayton had seemed to be sticking to him more closely. Clayton was always fascinated by Homer and loved nothing more than to follow him around, even if Homer was ignoring him. But a sleeping Homer had never held much interest for Clayton, and when Homer settled down for a nap, Clayton would usually hop off to find something else to do. For the past week, though, whenever Homer curled up on the couch to sleep, Clayton would lie down on the floor directly in front of him—not moving, not bothering Homer in any way. He'd just watch him intently without taking his eyes off him.

I hadn't thought much about it at the time, and I'd tried not to think at all about Homer's increased weariness. On the face of it, there wasn't even a connection between those two things. But it all came together in my mind now in a single, blurred rush.

"Oh, *Homer.*" I threw down my purse and ran to the couch. "Oh, my poor boy. My poor, poor boy." I gently released the

Homer and Clayton

two claws and sank to the floor, cradling him in my arms, my cheek pressed to the top of his head. "I'm sorry, Homer-Bear. I'm so sorry I wasn't here. I'm so sorry, little boy." I swayed back and forth, kissing his brow, as he lay inertly in my arms. "I'm so sorry, Homer-Bear. I love you so much." I placed him on the ground, on his own legs. He feebly took a few steps, then laid down, clearly spent from the effort.

I went outside on our balcony then. Pulling the sliding door firmly closed behind me, I began to sob—great, gasping heaves that seemed to start at my knees before being wrenched upward and out through my mouth. I cried for having been gone when Homer needed me, and I felt the pain of that, his pain, as a physical pain in my own body. I cried for all the times I knew I would cry about it again, that image of Homer hanging from the couch.

Countless times at unexpected moments, down through all the remaining years of my life. I cried for what I already knew in my heart even though I hadn't yet told it to myself in words. I cried for the blind kitten nobody had wanted, who'd come at a time in my life when I wasn't sure that anybody did, or ever would, want me. I cried for the last tangible link to those years of youth and uncertainty and discovery—a time that, even though it had since evolved into things infinitely better, was a vanished country now, one I could never return to. I cried for other things that would never come back, the greetings at the front door when I came home; the funny, sonar-like, sweeping turns of a little black head; the rattlesnake vibrating of an ecstatic tail (*Hooray! We're both here! We're together!*) that had been the first thing I'd seen every morning for sixteen years.

I cried for all of it, although the only articulate word in my head was, *Never.* It was suddenly the only word I knew. *Never. Never. Never.*

I had gone outside because I didn't want Homer to hear me cry like that, or Laurence for that matter. For their sakes, but also for my own. That first convulsion of grief was an animal thing, and instinctively I'd crawled away to hide my wound, to be alone with it. There was no one to hear me now but the buildings across the courtyard from ours. Their walls caught the sounds of my cries and sent them back to me, until the entire courtyard wailed in a Greek chorus of woe. *Alas! Alas!* I hung my head and arms over the balcony railing, pressing my hands over my eyes, and howled my loss to the empty courtyard below.

But I didn't allow myself to stay outside for more than a minute or two. I knew what had to be done, and I didn't want to give myself time to second-guess, to argue that maybe tomorrow would be better, that there might still be plenty of good days ahead. I had vowed that day when I'd spoken to Jackson, in preparation for just this moment, that I wouldn't wait until worse came to the absolute worst. I wouldn't wait until Homer wasn't Homer anymore before I let him go.

Months earlier, we'd found a vet who would be able to come to us at home when the time came. I had no intention of subjecting Homer to the animal hospital again, of making him spend the last moments of his life in the only place in the world of which he'd been starkly terrified. I spent the few hours before her arrival cuddling Homer in my lap and stroking his head in our old way. Laurence went out and got him a Popeye's chicken breast, which he mixed up with some turkey in Homer's bowl. Homer managed to make it from my lap as far as the bowl, but he was too tired to eat standing up and so ate reclining, like the Roman aristocrats of old. He did eat, though. He may not have cleaned his bowl, but he did eat.

The vet, when she came, was as kind as she'd sounded when I'd first spoken with her. She sat in the living room talking to Laurence and me about nothing in particular, until her presence among us stopped feeling awkward and ominous, and I was almost comfortable. Homer was lying in his spot at the end of the couch, close to her chair, and she affectionately stroked his head while she talked. He lay passively under her touch, although at one point he turned his head to press it into her hand.

Eventually, I picked Homer up and carried him into the bedroom, and the vet followed.

In the end, Homer died in his own home, in his own bed, in the arms of the person who'd loved him most. The vet left and quietly closed the bedroom door behind her after she'd given him the shot. I cradled Homer in my lap as I watched the muscles around the place where his eyes would have been relax into sleep for the last time. "*Eras mucho gato,*" I whispered into his ear. *Thou wert plenty of cat.*

It was, in its way, one of the most beautiful moments of my life. It was so beautiful that I couldn't even cry.

WHEN VASHTI DIED, WE scattered her ashes at Fort Tryon Park, far, far uptown in Washington Heights. It was a beautiful, hilly park with acres of wide lawns and lush flowerbeds, and it commanded stunning views of the Hudson River and the Palisades beyond. Vashti had always loved water, and I had wanted to give her a whole river of it, a place from which she could watch the water sparkle and dance before it was carried out to sea. Scarlett had never shared Vashti's love of water and grass, but we had brought her ashes there too, so that she could be with Vashti.

And so, a week later, when we received Homer's ashes, we carried them all the way up to Fort Tryon Park, to the same lawn beneath the same oak tree where we'd released Scarlett and Vashti. My original three—Homer and his first, fastest friends—would be together again. The views were as sun-dappled and peaceful as I remembered. I hoped, I wanted to believe, that Homer at last was able to see them, to see all the beautiful things in this world that he never had, even though he'd seemed to be born knowing them already.

There was hardly anybody else at the park that day, and Laurence and I were alone in our little spot. I kissed the wooden box holding Homer's ashes before I opened it. As if awaiting its cue, a breeze blew up and carried them away from us, into the sunlight and out toward the river.

I wish I could say that I had a stirring eulogy for the occasion, something as heroic and fine as Homer himself had been. Something befitting the send-off of a cat who had touched so many lives, who had become the symbol of something so much bigger than himself, but who had never stopped being my own, my much-loved, dear little guy.

But I had expended so many words on Homer already—tens of thousands of them. My words were all used up. I could only think of someone else's. A scrap of an E.E. Cummings poem I'd first read back in my college creative-writing days, when I couldn't possibly have foreseen the little black cat who would find me someday and become the author of all my good fortune.

"I carry your heart with me," I said to the air and the ashes and the water flowing below us. "I carry it in my heart."

The breeze waned, and Homer's ashes, which had risen high above our heads, began to fall into the waiting grass. Laurence and I took each other's hands, and then we turned to go.

The End of the Beginning

Do not go about with your cheeks all
covered with tears; it is not right that you
should grieve so incessantly.
-HOMER, *The Odyssey*

I WAITED NEARLY A week before I let Homer's onlIne community
know about his passing, needing time to mourn privately before
I could do so publicly. I had known that the response would be
overwhelming, although I didn't know then how overwhelming it
would be. The news about Homer grew and spread and then grew
more, changing our lives and Homer's legacy in ways we could
never have imagined.

But before I write about any of that, the time has come, as
promised, to write about Clayton and Fanny— how we adopted
them, what they brought to our family, and what they came to
mean to us. The last chapter of Homer's story is very much their
story, too.

WHEN I SET OUT to find a kitten to adopt as a companion for Homer, it was the first time I'd adopted a cat with a specific list of "qualifications" in mind. Actually, it was the first time I'd deliberately set out to adopt a cat at all.

Homer, Vashti, and Scarlett had all come into my life through a fortuitous combination of luck and circumstances and— while not generally a superstitious person—I'd believed in the karmic destiny of that, the sense that the cats I had been meant to love had found me, rather than vice versa. This was true even of the two older cats we'd tried out previously with Homer. And while things hadn't worked out permanently with our fosters, at least I'd been able to save them from certain death and help them find loving forever homes. Maybe that also was fate at work.

Now, however, we were looking for a kitten—not just waiting for one, but *looking*, because what Homer desperately needed after losing Scarlett was someone aside from Laurence and me to keep him company. The kitten ideally would still be very young—no older than two or three months, say—so that he or she would accept Homer's unusual face and particular ways without knowing that "normal" adult cats looked or acted any differently. I felt that we were uniquely suited to give a home to a kitten who had special needs. And, I soon realized, if we were going to adopt *one* young kitten, we should probably adopt *two*. Kittens were high energy, and a kitten with no one to play with besides Homer might drive him to distraction.

I entered my search parameters on Petfinder.com, and after a few clicks found myself looking at a picture of two kittens named Peeta and Katniss. They were a bonded pair of litter-mates with a foster network called Forever Friends—located deep in South Jersey, only an hour-and- a-half away by train—who hoped to adopt the two of them out together.

Both kittens were entirely black, although Katniss had a little locket of white fur just above her breastbone. Peeta had a deformed hind leg, more of a half- leg, really, which would likely have to come off at some point when he was older than the ten weeks he currently was. It didn't reach more than halfway to the ground and was of no use in propelling him forward when he walked, but he nonetheless uselessly spun and spun the half-leg as he moved, wasting energy and risking injury.

I knew as soon as I saw them that these were our kittens. The sun hadn't even come up yet when I filled out the online application, and I waited in a keyed-up state of anticipation for the hours to roll by until it was late enough for a (ahem) sane person to begin their workday and review the form I'd submitted. I received a call from Forever Friends before noon, and we talked for a while about Peeta and Katniss, their personalities, Peeta's special needs. I gave them a list of references, and a week later I stood on the platform of New Jersey Transit's Trenton station, waiting to meet the volunteer from Forever Friends who would deliver our newest family members.

Laurence and I had enjoyed the *Hunger Games* movies well enough, but ultimately wanted to name the kittens ourselves. Laurence chose Clayton for the boy, after the famous one-legged tap dancer Clayton "Peg Leg" Bates. I chose Fanny for the girl, simply because I thought it was a sweet, old-fashioned name, and in her pictures Katniss looked like a very sweet little girl.

Clayton and Fanny,
April 2012

WHEN FANNY AND CLAYTON came to us, it had been fifteen years since I'd lived with a kitten—and I'd never lived with litter-mates at all. I was charmed to see what a matched set they were, how they groomed each other lovingly and slept curled up in each other's bodies. Their faces had enough subtle differences to be distinguishable, yet the family resemblance was obvious. They had identical large, golden eyes, and a habit of sitting next to each other with their heads tilted at identical angles, regarding Laurence and me with identical wide-eyed, solemn gazes. It was adorable, yet at times could take on an almost eerie, *Children of the Corn* quality.

The most enduring early image I have of the two of them comes from the evening of their fourth day with us. We'd set them up in our guest bedroom at first, wanting to give them a chance to acclimate, to feel safe in their new space and to get used to things smelling like Homer, while also giving Homer a chance to get used to things—like the t-shirts I let them sleep on and then wore around the house—smelling like them.

On the fourth day, I opened the door to the guest room and let them out into the rest of the apartment for the first time. Clayton, as if shot from a cannon, immediately took off in a quick bunny-hop on his three good legs, down the long hallway and into the living room.

July 2012

Fanny, however, stood anxiously in the doorway to the guest room, crying for her brother to come back. Every few minutes, Clayton would hop back down the hall to where Fanny stood, touching his nose to hers in a reassuring way. *Come on! There's lots of cool stuff out here!* But he was too eager to see his new home to remain with her for long, and soon enough he'd scamper away again.

Much of what we came to learn about their personalities was reflected in those few minutes. Fanny was a fawn-like crea-ture—timid at first, easily spooked, but essentially composed of such pure sweetness and affection that it was like having Vashti with us again. It should be noted, however, that in terms of ap-pearance, Fanny was Vashti's exact inverse. Where Vashti had been a puffy white fluff-ball, Fanny's black, short-haired body grew long and slender as it took on the contours of adulthood. But she was, in her precisely opposite way, every inch the beauty Vashti had been. I liked to say that Fanny's face looked as if it had been drawn by Disney Princess animators, perfectly heart- shaped with high cheekbones, a slightly pointed chin, and tip-tilted almond eyes. "You're so pretty," Laurence would croon to her when he thought I couldn't hear. "You're a pretty, *pretty* girl." And, like Vashti be-fore her, Fanny would lean her head into Laurence's hand and gaze up at him adoringly. Perhaps because Fanny was so Vashti- like in so many of her ways, she and Laurence seemed to understand each other right from the start.

Fanny seemed to understand Homer immediately, too. She was intensely interested in him once she'd made it out of the guest room, but she always approached him gently and respectfully. She would wait until he'd finished cautiously sniffing her and seemed comfortable before attempting to touch her own nose softly to his. If Homer batted a crumpled ball of paper around the living room floor, she would bat it back to him but not otherwise try to intrude on his game until he'd come over and explicitly invited her to play. If Homer curled up on the couch, Fanny would also lie on the couch close enough to make Homer aware that he wasn't alone, but not so close as to make him feel crowded.

I don't think she understood that Homer was blind, per se, but she seemed to intuit that he was happiest when he could hear her coming. We'd bought belled breakaway collars for the kittens for just this reason. But Fanny always greeted Homer with a trilling coo, as an additional assurance that her approach was both imminent and friendly. As weeks passed and Homer began to revert to his former playful ways—to once again seek out mischief and fun and food as eagerly as he'd used to—it became clear that this was, at least in part, because Fanny was a balm on the wound that Scarlett's loss had left on Homer's spirit.

Clayton, on the other hand, was an intrepid little soul, ready of an instant to bound fearlessly and inquisitively at anything or anyone that crossed his path. Clayton darted down the hallway the day we opened the guest-room door for him, and he never stopped darting, never stopped exploring, never stopped trying to insert himself into everything going on around him. If I'd thought that Homer lacked even a concept of vision because he himself was unable to see, then Clayton seemed to lack even the idea that anyone might not like him, simply because he himself was utterly incapable of disliking anybody or anything.

I'll admit that Clayton was a puzzle to me for a long time. To say that cats are highly opinionated creatures is almost as reflexively obvious as saying that they have fur and whiskers. Even the most agreeable cat will have certain strong likes and dislikes. Fanny, for example, adored little toy mice and anything with feathers, but wasn't much interested in any other toys. She was passionate about cat foods made from lamb, duck, or tuna, but couldn't abide anything containing salmon or beef. As good-natured as Homer was, he hated being picked up, loathed being turned on his back, and would instantly recoil if you laid so much as a finger on his belly.

But Clayton liked everything. Literally *everything*. He liked crinkle balls and feathered toys and little fake mice and the plastic rings from water jugs and matchbooks and eyeglass cases and takeout menus and anything else small or portable enough for him to carry off in his mouth. He would eat anything you put in front of him. Dry or moist, regardless of flavor or texture—he ate everything and ate it all with equal gusto. You could pick him up, flip him over, rub his tummy, handle him however you liked, and he would nuzzle your hand and ask for more. One afternoon he sat in a chair with Laurence's visiting ten-year-old nephew, who (only for not knowing any better) spent nearly half an hour rubbing Clayton's fur the wrong way, while Clayton closed his eyes in a drowsy half-sleep, entirely unruffled.

Clayton liked everybody who came to our home and bunny-hopped out to greet them as fast as his three legs could carry him. He had a thick, club-like tail that swung out like a rudder at skewed angles behind him as he ran, most likely to compensate for some of the balance he lacked. When he wasn't running, however, his tail seemed stuck permanently in a happy, upward thrust, guaranteeing anyone who approached a friendly—a downright enthusiastic—reception.

Clayton even liked the vet. *He liked the vet!* A little cut at the bottom of his bad leg became infected and wouldn't heal, requiring the removal of that leg months ahead of our original schedule. There were a number of vet visits leading up to the surgery—and then the surgery itself—and Clayton not only didn't struggle or complain, he actually seemed to *enjoy* himself. When the vet pried back Clayton's lips to examine his gums and teeth, Clayton purred ecstatically. When the doctor stuck a needle into him to draw blood, Clayton butted his forehead playfully into the crook of the doctor's elbow. When he poked gingerly at the bottom of Clayton's infected half-leg—which, surely, must have been at least a little painful—Clayton flipped onto his back and bonked his whole head affectionately against the doctor while licking his hand. I couldn't help but feel somewhat vindicated at entering the same animal hospital where Homer had always caused such a ruckus with a *good* patient for a change.

But still...I wondered about things.

Fanny, as she grew, began to develop an adult cat's more complex vocal patterns—perhaps not as varied as Homer's, but deeper and more mature sounding than when she'd been only a few weeks old. Clayton, however, still had a very young kitten's undifferentiated, high-pitched squeak. His *meow* didn't even have an "ow" at the end. "*MEEEEEEEEeeee,*" he would say, starting out loud but trailing off as his breath ran out. "*MEEEEEEEEeeee,*" he said when I walked in the door, and, "*MEEEEEEEEeeee,*" he said when he wanted his food, and, "*MEEEEEEEEeeee,*" running to greet some new person, and, "*MEEEEEEEEeeee,*" when struggling for a plaything that was out of his reach. I joked that when the doctors had removed his bad leg, they'd taken away his "ow."

"There isn't any sign of...neurological damage, is there?" I asked the vet during one visit, just before Clayton's surgery. "Any developmental delays?"

He seemed baffled. "What do you mean? Like brain damage?"

"No," I said hastily. "Never mind. Just forget it."

Of course, Clayton was our veterinary practice's favorite cat, and whenever we came in there was a veritable welcoming committee waiting for us at the door. What a dream for a veterinarian—who presumably liked cats, yet only encountered cats who feared him—to finally find a cat who seemed positively thrilled in his presence. And what a dream for Clayton—who happily scamper-hopped around the exam table from the doctor to the vet tech and back again, demanding cuddles with a head-bonk and a high-pitched *MEEEEEEEEeeee*, hardly seeming aware of the needles, the rectal thermometer, or any of the other indignities to which he was subjected.

Perhaps the only thing Clayton didn't like was not having anyone around for him to like. It wasn't so much that he feared or disliked being alone. He simply never needed to be. Even Homer—much as he generally preferred to be with me—would *sometimes* head off to any empty bedroom or open closet. Fanny, sweet as she was and as much as she clearly loved us already, needed at least a few hours a day by herself, and would always prefer to be hidden away in some quiet spot when we had people over.

But Clayton never wanted to be alone, or even out of plain sight. Clayton didn't nap on top of chairs or under beds or buried among piles of clothing or tucked away in a corner of the closet. He'd sprawl out smack-dab in the middle of the floor of whatever room we were in, where you couldn't walk from one end of the room to the other without stepping over him. A question that, to this day, has literally never once been asked in our home is, *Where's Clayton? I haven't seen Clayton in a while.*

As I said, I loved Clayton right from the start—but he puzzled me. Part of the bond that we form with the animals we love comes from that sense that they know us, and that we know them, better than anybody else does or could. I never had—and never would—understand anybody down to the very bottom of their soul the way that I did Homer. I knew every like and dislike, every joy and fear, that Homer had, and had felt the first glimmers of that deep knowledge in those very earliest moments when we'd first met.

But what did I know about Clayton that any stranger couldn't have figured out within five minutes? What ultimately makes all of us different from each other— different and unique—are the things we like and the things we don't. Clayton liked everything and disliked nothing— or, if he did, he kept it to himself—which made him a bit inscrutable.

But if there was one thing that Clayton definitively liked more than anything else—one thing that could raise his usual level of happiness to outright ecstasy—that thing was Homer. Small as Homer was, he still towered over Clayton when we first adopted him—and Clayton clearly thought that Homer was the most fascinating thing in the whole world.

Clayton wasn't much interested in Homer when Homer was sleeping. But if Homer was awake and in motion then Clayton was right beside him. When Homer walked to his food bowl or the litter-box or down the hall, Clayton bunny-hopped along at his side. The pushiness of this—the lack of any respect for polite boundaries—irritated Homer at first. Every few steps, Homer would pause to whack Clayton in the face with one paw.

I don't know that Clayton *liked* being hit in the face by Homer, but it didn't seem to faze him, either. He'd crinkle his little brow a bit, but he never flinched or stepped back or raised his own small paw in a gesture of self-defense. He'd hop next to Homer or around him in circles, and every few feet Homer would pause to smack him in the face—and, like a Slinky, Clayton's head and neck would compress for a moment, then instantly spring back up.

Homer and Clayton together reminded me of Spike the Bulldog and Chester the Terrier from the old Looney Tunes cartoons. Spike would stride impressively down the sidewalk with little Chester scampering around him, peppering him with an endless stream of eager questions. *What are you doing, Spike? What are doing today? Where are you going, Spike? Huh? Can I come with you, Spike? Can I?* And every so often, without breaking stride, Spike would whack Chester in the face with a laconic, *Ehhh... shut up.*

That was Homer and Clayton to a T.

It pained me to see Homer bothered in any way, after the rough few months he'd had. But, ultimately, being irritated with Clayton was better than being sad about Scarlett. Homer began running and jumping again, at first to avoid Clayton, and then simply for the pleasure of it, as he'd used to do. If Fanny charmed and soothed him, then Clayton brought him out of his shell.

Scarlett and Vashti had never been as playful as Homer would have liked, and with them he'd never been able to assume a role more authoritative than that of mildly annoying little brother. Now Homer was the big brother, accompanied by two kittens who loved to play as much as he did and then some. He had reasons to get up from his spot on the couch, other than feeding times or his daily shift from the sofa to my lap. Clayton and Fanny were perfectly content to be minions and let Homer be the boss, and it was a role that Homer clearly relished.

Even if I hadn't been able to love them for their own sakes (and I was crazy about them—they were, as I would frequently say to Laurence, "made of adorable"), I would have loved Fanny and Clayton for bringing Homer back to me—*my* Homer, the Homer I knew and loved best, the Homer who'd always greeted each new day as something to celebrate. Homer was *Homer* again.

And I honestly believe that Homer wouldn't have found the strength he needed to fight his illness for as long as he did if not for these two ridiculously happy little ragamuffins, who moved into our home and claimed our lives for themselves.

HOMER HAD SOMETHING LIKE fifteen thousand followers on Twitter, but it was on Facebook and my blog where his real community lived. By now, there were nearly thirteen thousand people who'd "liked" Homer's Facebook page, but the number of people who actually followed us there on a day-to-day basis was still very small. They were the people for whom I posted pictures of Clayton and Fanny as they grew, and who had sincerely mourned with us when we'd lost our girls. Homer's community gave us the permission and space we needed to embrace our grief fully and recover at our own pace, without having to encounter a single person who rolled their eyes and wondered rather impatiently why we couldn't get over it already—why we were so sad when it was "just a cat."

I had known that the grief would be deeper, the sense of loss more profound, when we lost Homer. It was Homer's community, after all. But I had thought—naively, I now realize—that it would be more or less a slightly larger version of the same thing. Thinking this—that the one or two hundred comments and emails of condolence we had received after losing Vashti and Scarlett might be as many as four or five hundred now—I had waited four days after Homer's passing, enough time to put on a "game face," before posting the announcement to social media. It was August 25th—as fate would have it (although I didn't register this at the time), exactly four years to the day since *Homer's Odyssey* had first been published in 2009.

Publishing Homer's story had changed my life, but that change had been a slow one—because book publishing is a slow business. I'd spent nearly a year writing the proposal and outline for *Homer's*

Odyssey, another year finding a publisher and then writing the book itself, and it had been six months after *that* before the book had first appeared in hardcover. Even all the craziness of Homer's photo and video shoots had played out over a period of months, turning our lives topsy-turvy for perhaps one day every two or three weeks, and then leaving us to enjoy relative normalcy the rest of the time.

Nothing at all in my previous experience had prepared me for what it felt like to have my whole life change in a day.

The Facebook post announcing Homer's death was shared more than three thousand times, and received more than eight thousand comments, within only the first few hours. People began posting pictures and stories of their own special-needs rescue animals to Homer's page—animals they said they had been inspired to adopt by

An online memorial for Homer, August 2013

Homer's example. Most of them were cats—cats large and small, fluffy and hairless, former street cats, backyard cats, cats who had been considered "undesirable" by their breeders. Cats who were blind or deaf or both, or who were missing limbs or paralyzed from the waist down. "Wobbly" cats suffering from cerebellar hypoplasia, and cats who were positive for FIV or FeLV. There were also many special- needs dogs, a handful of rescued bunnies and horses, and one albino gecko with poor depth perception. (I swear I'm not making that up.)

I shared these pictures and stories with Homer's community as they came in, thinking them the most fitting tribute Homer could possibly have received. But for every one story and picture

I shared, three or four more would appear in the "Visitor Posts" column along the side of the page, until I could no longer keep up. And people posted other things, too. They found older pictures of Homer that I'd posted online years earlier, and they shared them again on Homer's page now. Sometimes they Photoshopped these pictures, to give Homer angels' wings, to show him at the Rainbow Bridge, to frame him with solemn black borders that announced the years of his birth and his death. Each photo and post moved me deeply—until a few days later, when the numbers were so large that I was simply bewildered. I hadn't known there were so many. I'd had no idea.

Facebook's algorithms clearly interpreted this influx of new activity on our page as "good," and began sending more and more and then even *more* traffic our way. It had taken nearly four years for Homer's page to accumulate those thirteen thousand "likes," to reach a point where content from the page reached perhaps five thousand people in a week. I had thought those numbers were pretty big. But, within a week of Homer's death, his page had acquired an additional fourteen thousand followers and reached more than two million people. Hour by hour, day by day, Laurence and I watched those numbers go up, thinking every day that surely—*surely*—today was the day when it would all begin to level off.

And every day we thought that, we were wrong.

When you lose a member of your human family, there's usually one day when you reach out to all the people who need to be called or notified, and then that part is done. But social media doesn't work that way. For all the thousands of people who'd seen my Facebook post within hours of its going up, there were many thousands more who didn't first see it in their news feeds for another day, or several days, or a couple of weeks. Every day there were people who were only now first seeing their friend's re-Tweet of somebody else's Twitter post that had gone up days ago. Every day somebody visited my website—not even knowing there was any specific news about Homer—and, reading my blog post for the first time, then forwarded it to half a dozen other people they knew, who themselves forwarded the link to a dozen more. Every day, somebody saw for the first time the share, re-tweet, or re-post of another blogger's tribute to Homer.

Sometimes the news was divorced from social media altogether—a rumor that people heard word-of-mouth, and they wrote to me for confirmation. At least twenty or thirty times in the typical day, I would receive emails from people wanting to know if what they'd heard was true, if Homer was really gone, and if so, when and how had it happened? For me, every day was the first day all over again.

I felt like a skipping record, forced to keep repeating the same notes over and over because my needle was stuck in a groove and couldn't get un-stuck.

Laurence has never said so, but I suspect that I wasn't exactly the world's greatest wife during this time. I know now that Fanny, and especially Clayton, felt a difference in me, too. I petted and played with them as much as I ever had, but something essential within me was becoming numbed.

The emails began pouring in immediately after I posted that first announcement, and within a few days they were followed by sympathy cards in the mail—first in a trickle, then in a gush, like something out of *Miracle on 34th Street*. We received hundreds—literally hundreds—of sympathy cards and letters, and hundreds more cards from shelters and rescue groups, informing us of donations that had been made in Homer's name. Along with the cards and letters, people sent us their own home-made versions of Homer—stuffed macramé Homers, ceramic Homers, Homers blown from black glass, a watercolor painting of Homer from Brazil, a Homer necklace pendant carved out of an old vinyl record from San Francisco, a hand-painted sculpture depicting a super-hero-caped Homer in front of the Twin Towers from Iowa, a soft-sculpture Homer purse that came all the way from Japan, a framed Homer needlepointed in black Egyptian silk and surrounded by gold thread from Los Angeles, and even an extravagantly framed oil portrait of Homer from "Hank For Senate's" humans in Virginia.

Soon the media inquiries followed. I ended up asking a book publicist I'd worked with once to write up a press release containing the essential facts and some boilerplate quotes from me, so that inquiring press could have something to work with without my having to tell the same story dozens of times. A few months later, *The New York Times Magazine* would run Homer's obituary online as part of December's annual "The Lives They Lived" feature, which rounded up notable deaths from the preceding year.

By then, enough time had passed for me to be proud and even a little amused, to wryly observe to Laurence that we certainly shouldn't expect the same kind of coverage when our time came.

But, at the time these things were happening, all I could think when dealing with press was that I was afraid of repeating the same things too often and sounding like a robot, yet also afraid of deviating from my stock answers and sounding like a moron.

I know how I sound in writing all this. *How* awful *it must have been for you, to receive the heartfelt love and sympathy of so many people!* It wasn't awful at all, of course. It was astounding, amazing, miraculous enough to convince even the most hard-hearted cynic of the generosity and infinite kindness people were capable of.

Every time somebody wrote to say that they felt as if Homer had been their own cat—that they'd cried upon hearing the news as if they'd lost one of their own—my own heart throbbed in sympathy. I knew—I *knew*—exactly how that felt. When I saw all the donations that had been made in Homer's name and thought of the lives that would be saved because of them, my heart swelled with gratitude. When I received all the beautiful things people made and sent to us, I was thankful until I thought my heart would burst with it.

And that was the problem—there was too much to feel and not enough me to feel it all. My life already felt strange and unlike my own life simply because Homer was no longer in it. But now, when I woke up, I would spend a good couple of hours walking around in a daze, not knowing how to pick up the thread of the day, where I should start, who I should call, which emails and inquiries and Facebook posts I was supposed to respond to.

Once my days had flowed along a natural, effortless rhythm that I didn't have to think about. Now I spent a half-hour each morning trying to decide when to take a shower. Did it make more sense to do a little work, then shower, and then get back to work again? Or would it be more logical and efficient to shower immediately, before I did anything else? Half the time I ended up not showering at all. Better to avoid the question altogether, I'd sagely conclude, rather than come up with the wrong answer.

I eventually realized that Laurence had seamlessly taken over most of the essential tasks that kept our lives running. It was Laurence who now fed Clayton and Fanny on their regular schedule. He also cleaned their litter-box, trimmed their claws, and fished their toys out from under the couch. Laurence prepared our meals and made sure I ate, kept us stocked with toilet paper and trash bags and toothpaste, wrote out checks for bills and made sure they were mailed on time.

All the gratitude, all the love, all the sorrow for the pain of others that I felt, overloaded me until all I felt was overwhelmed—overwhelmed and anxious, slipping further behind each day on all the thank-yous and acknowledgments I owed people, which continued to accumulate in new batches by the hour.

Somewhere, underneath this giant mound of *stuff* that had amassed atop me, was my grief for Homer. I had written about it, blogged about it, emailed Homer's mourners about it. But sometime in the midst of all that, at some point after we'd scattered his ashes and there was no physical, tangible task left for me to do, I'd lost my ability to feel it.

What I needed was to cry. I hadn't cried at all since that first wild convulsion of loss on the afternoon of the night when Homer had gone to sleep for the last time. Now I needed to shed the gentler tears of letting go. I had to get back to my grief in order to heal from it and move on.

But I couldn't. I couldn't find it. I didn't remember ever having felt as tired as I did now. I was too exhausted even to look.

My own life had been turned inside out, but as far as I could tell Clayton and Fanny were as happy as they'd ever been. They still ate big meals and napped together in sunbeams, still chased crinkle balls and the laser pointer's ever-elusive red dot with the same joyous abandon. When I piled all the sympathy cards and letters we'd received into the middle of the living room rug—hoping to create some semblance of order from them—Clayton would dive right into the middle of the pile, burrowing into and under it as if he were a child in a ball tank.

It was a few weeks later, in late September, when I noticed one evening that Clayton was having trouble with his litter-box, hopping in and out of it more frequently than was usual. When I checked, however, he didn't seem to be producing anything. I assumed that he was a little blocked, and I added some olive oil to his moist food for an evening meal. He gobbled the whole thing down with his typical enthusiasm, which I found reassuring.

Later that night, however, it was a different story. Clayton was in and out of his litter-box every few minutes now, his pupils hugely dilated. When he wasn't in the litter-box, he paced back and forth across the living room in an odd fashion, crouching first in one random spot, then another.

I had been planning to take him to his regular vet the next morning if the problem persisted. But he seemed so *very* uncomfortable—and was acting in so very unusual a way—that I didn't want to make him wait another eight hours for relief. If it had been Homer, who'd hated the vet with a furious passion, I might have taken a more wait-and- see attitude. But Clayton didn't mind doctors, and even though it was 11:00 and our animal clinic was closed for the night, I thought, *Better safe than sorry.* So, bundling him into his carrier, and waiting for Laurence to grab a jacket so he could accompany us as far as the sidewalk and see us safely into a cab, I headed for the 24-hour emergency animal hospital on West Fifteenth Street.

The last time I'd been in a cab ferrying a cat to an emergency room had been with Homer, and that had clearly been a life-or-death situation. It didn't feel like that this time, though. I still believed the problem was constipation—albeit clearly a severe case—because, in my range of experience with cat maladies, I hadn't yet encountered anything else that seemed to match these symptoms. Vashti's CRF had caused her to be constipated from time to time, and Clayton's behavior now wasn't completely dissimilar to what hers had been then.

Vashti's physical inverse, Fanny, may have been sleek and slender, but Clayton was mushy in the middle. He was a bit of a food hound, and had a habit—one we couldn't break—of finishing his own meals and then tackling Fanny's. Fanny was always obliging enough to allow him to do so. She was a healthy weight, according to her doctor, and even when I'd secretly put down some extra food for her when Clayton wasn't looking, she didn't seem particularly interested. So I assumed now that Clayton had eaten too much of something that didn't agree with him, and my heart ached with sympathy for his obvious discomfort. I reached my hand through the top of his cloth carrier to stroke his head reassuringly. *Poor kitty,* I crooned. *Poor Clayton.* But I also murmured, with a kind of rough affection, *Maybe now you'll learn your lesson, and let poor Fanny eat her meals in peace.*

The emergency animal hospital on West Fifteenth was the polar opposite of our regular clinic—a cavernous, fluorescent-lit waiting area studded with row after row of hard-backed chairs. It was close to midnight, and the only other person in the enormous space was a man with a huge German Shepherd, who'd just finished being sick all over the spotless linoleum floor. Another man in a blue orderly's uniform hurried over with a mop and push-bucket, while the man with the dog patted his flank in a soothing way, helping him into an exam room in the back. The woman at the check-in desk took Clayton's name, the reason for our visit, and my credit card information with brisk efficiency. We didn't have to wait more than a few minutes before a doctor approached and summoned us into an exam room of our own.

Clayton didn't struggle as the vet lifted him from his carrier, but he did mewl in a pained, pathetic way when her hands first went under his belly for support, then gently probed his lower abdomen. I couldn't remember ever hearing

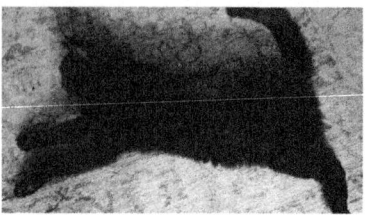

Clayton, 2013

Clayton make a sound that wasn't *happy*. And, for the first time, I felt the stirrings of fear in my own belly.

"Have you noticed any blood in his urine?" she asked.

"No." The question startled me. *His urine?* "You don't think it's constipation?"

She removed the little blanket lining Clayton's carrier and spread it onto the exam table, so that Clayton could lie down more comfortably. "I think he has something called feline idiopathic cystitis," she said. "It's a blockage of the urinary tract. It's life-threatening if we don't catch it in time, although," she hastily assured me, "it's highly treatable when we do. We call it 'idiopathic' because we don't really know what causes the condition. Generally we think it's brought on by stress. Have there been any significant changes in your home recently?"

At first, the combination of the words *stress* and *Clayton* in the same sentence struck me as so absurd that it was almost comical. Was any cat ever *less* prone to stress than Clayton was?

But then, unbidden, a memory came back to me. When the vet had come to us on Homer's last day, she'd wrapped him in a blanket when it was over, leaving only his face revealed. She'd then placed his body tenderly in a bag she'd brought with her—a roomy leather bag with handles.

The bag containing Homer had remained opened and unzipped on the floor while I signed papers and made arrangements for the cremation. And Clayton had climbed into it. I'd thought it merely the natural curiosity of any cat to explore an open bag left on the floor. But, when we'd tried to lift him out, Clayton had clung to the blanket around Homer, whining anxiously as we'd fought to pull him away.

Grief has a way of making us selfish. As many people as had mourned for Homer—and as sincere and deep as I'd known that mourning to be—I'd been sure that nobody's loss could equal my own. Homer had been *my* cat, his loss had been *my* loss—and there was no one, I thought, who could truly know how I felt.

Clayton lay on the exam table between the doctor and me, the gold of his eyes dulled from their usual bright alertness. But when I placed my hand down on the table next to him, he laid one small, black paw over it and looked up into my face.

I had been wrong. There *had* been another who'd known how I felt. Someone else had felt his happily ordered world run off course, had lost his hero and very best friend, not understanding *why* that friend was gone and couldn't come back to play with him anymore.

He just hadn't known how to tell me.

My voice was gritty when I spoke. "Our oldest cat..." The words stuck, and I realized that, for all the blogs and emails and Facebook posts, I hadn't actually said it aloud to anyone. Not once. Not in all this time.

I cleared my throat and tried again. "Our oldest cat died a few weeks ago. Clayton was very attached to him." I felt the relief of saying it—just saying it as a commonplace statement, to a person who didn't know Homer or that I was "Homer's mom," who would greet the idea with nothing more than ordinary, professional sympathy—pass through me. It felt like having a rusty gate you'd been pushing and pushing against finally begin to swing open, just a crack.

"I'm so sorry," the vet said. "That could certainly do it."

"But Clayton will…" I cleared my throat a second time. "He will be okay, right? I did get him here in time?" *Not again,* I thought. *Please not again, not now, not so soon…*

"I think he'll be fine," she replied. "He'll have to stay with us for two or three days so we can clear the blockage and get everything flowing the way it should. Let me take him back now and get him started. You can wait up front for the receptionist to bring the papers you'll need to sign."

Clayton was away for three days. I'd always gone to visit our other cats when they'd had overnight hospital stays. When Clayton had his leg removed, I'd seen him at least once a day. He'd had to stay for two weeks then, so he could be crated while his stitches healed. It was impossible to imagine otherwise how we would have kept a rambunctious kitten stable enough not to risk the stitches—or how we would have kept Fanny, who groomed him daily, from going after them herself. Keeping Clayton crated at home—in full view of the rest of us interacting with each other, but not with him—had seemed unnecessarily torturous.

But I'd gone to see him every afternoon and brought him treats. And the doctor and other staff members had taken him periodically into an empty exam room for brief bouts of closely supervised play. He'd seemed nothing but happy when I'd visited him then, surrounded by toys that he batted around playfully when he was in his cage, and by adoring humans during the brief times he was allowed out of it.

This time, however, the hospital asked that I not come and visit. It was important that Clayton remain hooked up to tubes and catheters around the clock, and unhooking him long enough for a visit from me was, I was told, an undesirable option. I called three times each day to check on him, and at a minimum I knew that Clayton was still the easy patient, as compliant with staff as he'd always been. The day when I finally went to bring him home, a tech handed over his carrier and informed me, "Clayton is the most adorablest cat ever." Which told me that his usual sunny charm must have returned during those three days, at least in part.

I was given a sheet with after-care instructions, a case of a new prescription food, and a bill so steep that I almost reeled. (An emergency animal hospital in Manhattan possibly being the most expensive option for veterinary care anywhere on the planet.) It was worth it, though, as I saw Clayton's soft carrier pop like popcorn when he heard my voice, and realized that I had come back for him.

Clayton was overjoyed to be released from that carrier once we got home—although taken aback by Fanny's hostile reception. He may have *looked* like the Clayton she knew, but he *smelled* like something else altogether, and Fanny backed up and hissed at him angrily whenever he approached. I quickly brought Clayton into our bedroom, which I'd set up ahead of time with a new litter-box, his favorite toys and blankets, and a bowl for his new food. If stress had caused his illness, I didn't want his recovery set back by the additional stress of rejection. Within a few days, I knew, Clayton would smell like himself again, and he and Fanny could fall back into their established patterns of close companionship.

Laurence came in every so often to check on us, and Clayton scampered over to bonk his head joyously against Laurence's hand as he bent down to scratch behind Clayton's ears. *Look! I'm back! I'm finally home!* But otherwise Clayton and I were alone together for the rest of the night. He bunny-hopped frenetically around the bedroom for a long time, thrilled to be released from the confinement of the hospital, delighted to reacquaint himself with his favorite toys, which he chased with dizzying speed over and under the bed, from one end of the room to the other. Every few minutes he'd jump into his litter-box, releasing a few small dribbles each time, which would have alarmed me if his doctor hadn't told me to expect this for a day or two.

It was late by the time he'd finally exhausted himself. Switching off the bedside lamp, I crawled beneath the covers and readied myself for sleep. I'd set up a soft pile of blankets and pillows on the floor for Clayton, as he'd never really been a cuddler or expressed much interest in sharing our bed. As friendly as he could be, Clayton wasn't a lap cat. If I sat on the floor, he'd hop around me in counter- clockwise circles, bumping his head affectionately against my shoulder or back as he went, pausing on occasion to rest in my lap for the briefest of seconds before leaping up and resuming his bunny-hop circles.

I'd never expected that any of our cats would cuddle on demand—Scarlett would certainly have disabused me of any such notion a long time ago. Still, one of the things I missed most about Homer was no longer having a furry little body to curl up with. I missed that feeling of peace that comes only when a small animal trusts you enough to fall asleep in your arms.

So it surprised me, as I got under the blankets, when Clayton climbed onto the bed after me. And then he did something he'd never done before. Hopping across the bed to where I lay, he nosed the covers aside and stretched his body across mine, one hind leg tucked beneath my right arm, while his front paws sprawled out to touch my left. His chest was directly over my chest, his heart aligned with my own. My arms rose from the bed to embrace him, and Clayton nuzzled his nose into my neck, purring gently against my left ear.

It was then—at last, at long last—that my tears began to flow. Not the harsh animal sobs of the day I'd lost Homer, but something infinitely softer than that, an easing, a warm, fluid salt. Clayton's weight was heavy on my chest, and yet it felt lighter than it had in weeks, as if it were emptying out as the tears ran down my cheeks. They mingled with Clayton's black fur as he brought his head to mine and, with exquisite patience, licked the tears from my skin with his raspy tongue, as the soft thrum of his purrs rumbled against my ear.

Baby boy, I whispered. *My little baby boy.*

I wept for Clayton, for having nearly lost him. I wept for the relief of holding him again now, safe and healthy and returned to us.

And I shed the tears I'd needed to shed for so long— for Homer, so that I could finally let him go.

Homer may have been the blind one, but I'd been the one who couldn't see. I had tended to dismiss Clayton's simplicity—the ease with which he found joy in absolutely everything around him—as simple-mindedness. I had thought it incompatible with depth of feeling. Sometimes (it shamed me to admit), I'd wondered if, perhaps, Clayton wasn't very *smart*.

But Clayton knew things that I didn't know—things, I realized, that Homer had known also. Perhaps that was why Clayton had clung so fast to Homer from his first day in our family, refusing to leave Homer's side even for a moment, not even at the end.

Clayton was always happy because happiness was an essential pre-condition of his life. Everybody wants happiness, and everybody tries to capture and hold it, and everybody feels the emptiness when it's gone. But Clayton spun everyday life into happiness—all of it, even the bowl of food that might not be his favorite flavor, or the unpleasantness of shots at the vet's office—the way trees turn

sunlight into food, without thinking, without any deep philosophy, but as a reflexive action, simply because without it, they can't
live.

In this, he was infinitely lucky.

When Homer left us, it was the first time in Clayton's short life
something had happened that he couldn't spin into happiness, and
he had despaired. But now, returning home after the three days in a
cold, impersonal hospital, feeling loving arms around him, feeling
healthy after days of being sick, he was happy once again.

I may have understood that his happiness was only the flip side
of his sadness, that it only existed *because* of that sadness—but all
Clayton knew was that he was happy, now, in this moment. Happy
and loved. And that was enough.

Much like Homer had taught me things about life—things so
simple that I should have figured them out on my own, yet might
never have without him—Clayton was teaching me something
now. I learned from him that happiness sometimes leaves, but that
it does come back— even if it comes in a different form than the
one you've lost. Loss wasn't scorched earth. It was a clay from
which good things could grow—things that were strange and different from what had come before, things it might never have even
occurred to you to want, but things you couldn't bear to part with
once you had them.

Even if you knew you'd only gained those things by losing others
that you'd have killed and died to keep forever.

THESE ARE ALL FINE, lofty-sounding ideas. But for me—for me,
personally—they form the very real substance of my everyday life.

At the time of Homer's death, his Facebook page had rough-ly thirteen thousand followers. Today, only two years later, that number is nearly 750,000 and counting. Having such a large au-dience isn't just a "cool" thing. It's a mighty thing. Shelters write to me about special-needs animals who've been with them for years, who they can't find homes for, and Homer's community gets the word out and finds them homes within days, making way for new rescues and additional lives to be saved. "Homer's Heroes" have raised hundreds of thousands of dollars to save the lives of animals in the wake of disasters both large and small across the globe. Everything from earthquakes and tsunamis to hoarding situations, or fires at shelters so tiny and volunteer-run that they don't have a single official employee. In July of this year alone, Homer's Heroes raised over forty thousand dollars to save animals in Nepal, cats being hoarded in West Virginia who stood in danger of being destroyed, and lions on a wildlife preserve in Africa. All of the money comes from small, individual donations, and one hundred percent of the funds go directly to those for whom the funds were raised.

People share their own rescue stories on Homer's page, rescues that occur in quiet, out-of-the-way places against seemingly im-possible odds. Stories that inspire others to try a little harder, to save a life they might not have thought could be saved, to give a chance to an animal whose chances might otherwise have appeared exhausted.

The greatest gift Homer left me with when he left me for good was fresh evidence every day—every single day—of the innate goodness of most people, even when news headlines make it far too easy to conclude otherwise.

In a very literal way, Homer's passing brought life in its wake. There are countless animals alive today because of Homer's loss, and the community that grew and flourished from our shared grief—which doesn't make it "worth it," but does assure me that even in his physical absence, Homer's spirit hasn't gone anywhere.

As I write this, Fanny is doing her best to insert her head between my hands and the keyboard, and Clayton is lying in my lap, flipped onto his back with one paw reaching up in his sleep to touch my face. It's a gesture that's become everyday for us, but one that never fails to knock me out anew with all the profound trust and serenity it implies.

Clayton and I might never have found each other if we hadn't lost Homer. And as much as I know that if I could wave a magic wand and undo Homer's death, I would do so in a heartbeat—in a nanosecond—I also know that I would never trade any of the things I have in my life today because I loved Homer, and also because I lost him.

Not for worlds.

SPRAY ANYTHING

MORE TRUE TALES OF HOMER AND THE GANG

GWEN COOPER

Love in a Cold Climate

IT WAS JANUARY OF 2001, and every job interview I had in New York started with the same question: "You want to move to New York—in *January*—from Miami Beach?"

Sometimes this would be followed by the interviewer rhapsodizing about how his or her secret dream was making the reverse move of the one I contemplated—from Manhattan to South Beach instead of vice versa. Sometimes reference would be made to the temperature, currently hovering in the twenties in New York City, thermometers struggling to rise beneath a thick blanket of slate-gray clouds that wouldn't let a single ray of sunshine through, yet also stubbornly refused to yield the gentle snowfall that might have cloaked the city in a hint of romance. Sometimes the interviewer would simply wave a hand to indicate a frost-covered window—which, to my benighted eyes, looked glittery and dazzling, the secret, overnight work of the snow fairies I'd read about in books as a child. But to the typical New Yorker, it meant only one thing: *It's freaking COLD out there!*

Always, however, the question would be asked in the sort of incredulous, are-you-*crazy?!* tone only a true New Yorker can muster—as if I'd announced that, after the interview, I intended to treat myself to the finest Italian meal New York City had to offer...at the Times Square Olive Garden.

South Beach, where I currently lived, was the land of bare skin and beaches—of white sands, turquoise waters, and year-round tans. My apartment building boasted an Olympic-sized swimming pool, which could be comfortably enjoyed for all but perhaps two uncharacteristically cold weeks out of the year. A mere thirty feet from that pool was Biscayne Bay, where one could go boating or jet skiing even (and especially) in the depths of January. From the balcony of my spacious one-bedroom apartment, I could look to the left and see the Bay, and to the right I could see the ocean itself, its waters closest to shore dotted with puffy white windsurfing sails and colorful floats upon which sunbathers bobbed along and, a bit farther out, the occasional cigarette boat zooming along, leaving a barely discernible wake.

Only a truly insane person, the raised eyebrows of my interviewers strongly implied, would consider trading this paradise for the purgatory of New York City in winter.

"Hell is hot all year round, too," I'd quip, "but nobody wants to live there." By this, I didn't mean to imply that my life in South Beach could be described as "hellish." Far from it. But I did feel—with all the confidence of a person who'd never had to stand a truly cold climate for more than five consecutive days in her entire life—that warm weather wasn't everything. Like a person who's always been so wealthy that she truly can't understand why people make such a fuss about *money*, of all things, I took sunshine and soft, salt-scented breezes for granted. I didn't think it was *nothing*, but it hardly made sense to arrange one's whole life around so trivial a consideration.

I wasn't a masochist, and the decision to move to New York wasn't one I'd arrived at lightly. I didn't work in tourism, hospitality, or international finance—just about the only stable industries in Miami. I worked in corporate marketing communications and, since I didn't have a background in any of the aforementioned fields, my only real job opportunities had come from the kind of fly-by-night companies that sprang up like dandelions and disappeared just as quickly from Miami's ever-shifting economic landscape. I wanted to work for a media company—print or online ("online" still being a fairly new word in the common parlance), it didn't matter to me. I wanted to work with people who created written content for a large audience, and I had a vague hope that I, myself, might someday be one of those people who created that written content.

Plus, I'd always been more partial to cityscapes than beachscapes, anyway. I loved tall buildings, small sidewalk cafes, live theater, and quirky little shops that weren't part of a national chain. In my mind's fanciful eye, I saw myself with chic coats and jackets, sweaters in my closet (a closetful of sweaters—imagine it!) that varied in thickness, so that some made more sense for the early days of fall while others were clearly best suited for the late days of winter. I imagined suede boots with high heels that would rap confidently along concrete sidewalks, adding two—or perhaps even three—inches to my height.

There's no such thing as "living" in New York—there's only surviving there, a writer friend of mine, a New York transplant to Miami, had warned me. But I pooh-poohed the notion. New York was where I wanted to be. My twenty-ninth birthday had just passed, and my thirtieth was looming on the horizon—which meant there was no better time than the present.

I ended up receiving a few job offers, one of which came with the added bonus of covering my moving expenses. The die was cast. On January 29th of 2001, just over two weeks before Valentine's Day, my three cats and I moved from our roomy South Beach one-bedroom into a small studio in Manhattan.

THE COLD WAS BEWILDERING to all of us at first—my cats as well as me. It howled around our new corner apartment way up on the thirty-first floor. You could actually hear the cold wind whipping around outside our windows at night as if demanding to be let in, which caused the four of us to shiver closer together (or as close as the ever-aloof Scarlett would allow the other cats to get to her) beneath the thick comforter I'd packed into an extra checked suitcase on our plane ride up.

Vashti, out of all of us, was perhaps genetically best suited for cold weather, with her thick snowy fur and the tufts of white that sprang from beneath the pink pads of her paws, like built-in snowshoes. But even she was stunned into a certain sluggishness for the first few days, the three of them—including Homer, usually such a little bundle of activity—spending most of their time either sleeping or wandering around the confines of our new, tiny apartment in a disoriented way, territorially staking out warm spots on the floor for the hour in the mornings when sunlight (if it wasn't cloudy) fell directly through the windows.

Homer was particularly confused by the fact that we were now living in a single room, a turn of events that not only didn't jibe with anything in his previous experience, but which was, apparently, beyond even his conceptual understanding. He seemed convinced there was a door that would lead to another room, somewhere, if only he could find it, whining and pawing fretfully at the plaster whenever his nose or whiskers encountered a wall where it seemed clear to him that a door ought to be.

Scarlett and Vashti, unlike Homer, could *see* that our new apartment was, indeed, as small as it felt. They could also tell that the sound of the wind outside wasn't made by an actual creature seeking entrance. But not so with Homer. Sometimes I woke in the night to hear him hiss in alarm as a particularly strong gust of wind tore loudly around the outside of our walls. *Stay out! We don't need any more cold in here!*

It didn't help that our heater—which should have been able to ward off any feeling of cold inside, even if it couldn't stop the sound of it outside—periodically made a startlingly loud buzzing sound, and then clanked and clonked four or five times, before releasing (evidently with great reluctance) a hiss of warm air into the room. *Buzzzzzzzz! Clank! Clank! CLONK! hissssssss*, went the heater, always provoking my over-protective Homer into wild frenzies of hissing and clawing at he-knew-not-what (some unidentifiable monster who, for inexplicable reasons, had moved in with us, I always imagined him thinking). One time he landed a full-clawed blow on the heater's metal grating and his paw remained stuck there, a single claw lodged in the grate and refusing to budge, and I had to come to his aid. Knowing nothing about heaters—having literally never lived with one before—it took me about a month longer than it should have to realize that this wasn't normal heater behavior, and to call the super to come up and replace it. By then it was March, and the weather was starting to turn warmer anyway. But for that first month, I ended up switching the heater off much of the time, preferring even the cold to all the racket.

It also didn't help that we were living in our New York apartment for more than two weeks before our furniture was finally delivered from Miami. I had ditched quite a few pieces (most notably a loveseat and dining set) before my move, since I wouldn't have been able to come close to fitting everything from my old place into my new one. The resulting shipment was so small, it wasn't worth the moving company's time to bring it up north until they were able to combine it with another. (Apparently, there were at least two of us half-baked enough to move from Miami to New York in the winter.) In the meantime, I had to make do with an air mattress that kept mysteriously deflating over the course of the night, causing me to wake up with aching bones atop a pancake-flat rubber swath that was the only cushion between my joints and cold, hardwood floors. I nearly blinded myself, so closely did I scrutinize every millimeter of that air mattress, looking for even the smallest tear or hole that I could patch up. I never found one, though, and so had to continue camping out on the cold floors of the "luxury" apartment I was paying far too much to live in, all things considered.

The cats fared slightly better at night than I did, able to curl up on top of me, or on some particularly thick wedge of the quilt, and find comfort that way. We all became very close those first weeks. Vashti, in particular, was fond of draping herself across my neck at night like a boa. I'd awaken from dreams of being smothered by giant marshmallows during a prison riot (dreams fueled by a particularly loud *Clank! Clank! CLONK!* from the heater) to find that Vashti's luxurious plume of a tail had fallen across my mouth and nose while we'd slept. Once, before I was fully awake, I ended up inhaling rather a sizeable wad of Vashti's tail fur through my open mouth and then spent the rest of the subsequent workday, to my eternal embarrassment, struggling with the resultant hairball that had lodged in my throat. "Are you okay?" various cowork-ers asked in concerned tones, as I coughed and retched my way through meetings. "Seasonal allergies," I claimed weakly, once I'd stopped wheezing long enough to squeeze out of a few words. I'm not sure that they believed me, but anything was better than saying, *Don't mind me—I'm just coughing up a hairball!* "How do you guys *live* with this?!" I demanded of my cats when I got home that night. I'd often said that my fondest wish would be to come back in a future life as one of my own pampered cats—but if hairballs were part of the deal, I found myself thinking now, I might have to reconsider.

I spent a lot of time talking to my cats during those early days right after my move—simply because there wasn't much else to *do*. There was nothing at all in my apartment aside from the deflating air mattress, my comforter and two pillows, a couple of books, a clock radio, a telephone, a litter box and food bowls—and, of course, my cats. After nightfall—which, its being February, occurred well before I got home from work—light came from the overhead bulbs in the kitchen and bathroom, left on continu-ously until I went to sleep. Still, there wasn't much light in the apartment except for the spot directly under the kitchen's fluores-cent, which made reading a book challenging unless I propped my back against a cabinet while sitting on the cold tile of the kitchen floor—not exactly a comfortable position to settle into for a few hours with a good novel.

The cats' eyes glowed from the shadows of our mostly dark apartment, and I often sensed that they reflected a hint of accu-sation. *Why did you move us to this cold, empty place? We were so happy where we were!* "Hey—it's hard for me, too!" I said aloud, more than once, which was usually about the time I realized that I needed to hear a human voice if I were to get through the rest of the long night ahead. I'd pick up the phone to call friends still back in South Beach, lounging poolside or preparing to head out to the launch party for one or the other of this year's hot new SoBe clubs, which was invariably opening in what had formerly been the site of one of last year's hot new SoBe clubs.

It was precisely what I'd frittered away too much of my twenties doing—what I'd moved to New York to get away from as I charted a new, more serious path into my impending thirties. So there was really no reason, I'd remind myself, to feel as homesick as I did during these conversations, pulling one of my cranky cats into my arms and stroking them until the build-up of static electricity in their fur—created by the cool, dry air of our new home—forced me to stop. That I even found myself missing Miami's oppressive humidity was a sign of how homesick I was. Sure, all the moisture in the air had frequently left me with a tangle of frizzy curls that looked as if it should have adorned the head of a circus clown. But at least I'd been able to pet my cats as much as I wanted without having to worry about shocking them into hostility.

I always ended up cutting these phone calls short, and the friend I was talking to would always promise, "I'll tell everyone you send your love!" before hanging up. Then I'd turn on my static-y clock radio, to relieve the dead silence of our apartment way up on the thirty-first floor, and release my equally static-y cat. He or she would run off to pass a static-electric shock to a resentful brother or sister, who'd recoil reproachfully (*Hey! What was that for?!*) at the little spark that flew between them when their noses touched.

BOTH THE COLD AND the sheer, overwhelming size of the city I now officially lived in were intimidating and conspired to keep me indoors for the first few days. But I couldn't spend all my non-work hours sitting alone in a dark apartment, and so I began taking long walks at night and on the weekend. I was trying to figure out Manhattan's byzantine subway system (legend has it that there's still no entirely accurate map of all its tunnels and stops) and, standing on platforms and waiting for trains to arrive, blasts of cold air would whip through the tunnels, blowing my hair back, whenever a train was about to make an appearance. The old leather bomber jacket my father had handed down to me before I'd left Miami was no match for the cold outside. I also lacked gloves or a good, thick scarf, and even the handful of sweaters I'd accrued over the years in Miami weren't as warm as I would have liked. *It'll be different next winter,* I'd tell myself. *Next year, I'll be able to afford everything I need.* For now, though, there wasn't much I could do beyond stamping my feet and breathing warm air onto my hands as I rubbed them together, before shoving them into the too-large pockets of my dad's old jacket, which still let in entirely too much cold air for comfort.

And yet, it was undeniably exciting to walk around this sprawl-ing, hectic, over-stimulating urban landscape I now called home. The buildings and shop windows all lit up at night like Christmas trees, promising the warmth inside that was denied to those of us outside on the pavement. Crowded as they were, though, with masses of people scurrying frantically to and fro, the pavements of Midtown were still warmer than they were down in the Fi-nancial District, where I lived, which almost completely emptied out after five o'clock. Walking through Soho on a sunny Saturday afternoon—thronged with trendy weekend shoppers, even in the middle of February—it was almost possible to forget how cold it truly was.

I was delighted to find, as I rambled along with no particular destination, small bodegas and bookstores that actually had "shop cats" in residence. I'd never encountered shop cats in Miami, and finding an ordinary place of business that had a cat dwelling in its inner recesses felt like discovering some hidden world, accessible only to a select few who knew where to look. And I also found more small, quirky pet stores than I would have thought one city could hold. My shopping for pet supplies back home had primarily taken place in superstores like Petco and PetSmart, whereas here in New York there was an endless array of mom-and-pop options—each with its own distinct personality and brand of shop clerks, ranging from morose hipsters, whose sulky expressions clearly conveyed that they were bored out of their wits, to comfortable-looking middle-aged cat ladies who were more than happy to engage in earnest conversations about which food or toy might best suit a particular cat's health needs and personality. I felt like a true New Yorker—a tribe famed for being short of temper and long on opinions—the Sunday morning when I got into a heated argument with the proprietor of an all-vegan pet shop as to whether it was healthy, or even possible, to feed cats, obligate carnivores as everyone knows, an all-vegan diet. (It's not, and you shouldn't.) To this day, that store remains the one and only retail establishment from which I've ever been banned for life. As if, I haughtily informed the righteously indignant proprietor, I would even *think* of visiting *that* store again.

Most of my encounters were far more positive, however. I was constantly finding little things to bring home for the cats—exotic new flavors and varieties of cat treats, imaginatively decorated brands of canned food that I'd never encountered back in Miami.

I bought little bags of catnip and three heated cat beds that could be plugged into the wall—so that the cats would have something warm and soft to sleep on, even if I didn't. My reward was the first genuine demonstration of feline contentment I'd seen since the move, as all three of my cats rolled around on their backs in custom-heated ecstasy, high on warmth and the 'nip I'd sprinkled judiciously all over the soft plush before plugging the cat beds in.

I even bought a new kitty condo, which all three of them could climb to the top of (and finally have something to perch on in our new place), although only Vashti and Scarlett could ascend its heights and then peer down from the tops of our tall windows on the thirty-first floor to take occasional, pointless swipes at birds flying by, or gaze down like all-powerful gods on the antlike humans scurrying about far below them.

I guilt-shopped more than I should have for the cats, filling my apartment full of cat stuff as a substitute for the actual furniture I still hadn't been able to make materialize, despite near-daily phone calls to the moving company. A stranger visiting my apartment—and seeing my deflated air mattress, shoved into one corner with my comforter and pillows like a rat's nest, and then taking in all the cat toys and cat beds and the new cat condo—would likely have concluded that I was some sort of crazy cat lady who'd "gone to the mattresses" while lamming it from mafia hitmen.

Perhaps the only disheartening thing about all the time I spent out of doors—aside from the cold itself, which was brutal and unrelenting—were the festive windows of jewelry stores and card shops and restaurants, all proclaiming the imminent arrival of Valentine's Day. I would be alone this year—utterly alone in a way I never had been before. It wasn't as if I'd left some great boyfriend behind in Miami (had there been a great boyfriend, I likely wouldn't have moved away in the first place). And it certainly wasn't as if I'd never before borne witness to excited women in my office whose desks, for that one day, were adorned with colorful bouquets and heart-shaped boxes of candy while my own desk remained bare of all such baubles. I'd never even really cared all that much about Valentine's Day, truth be told—not even when I'd had boyfriends to spend the holiday with.

But this would be the first year when I wouldn't have the option of hanging out with a group of friends—to watch a marathon of rom-coms (if we were feeling aspirational) or action movies (if we felt like going against the romantic mood of the day)—while we reassured each other that we were all fabulous and would eventually be appreciated by The Right Person, who simply hadn't materialized yet, and that everybody knew Valentine's Day was just a made-up Hallmark holiday, anyhow. I was still young enough to feel that arbitrary calendar dates amounted to milestones against which I was supposed to be measuring my progress in life—and this last Valentine's Day of my twenties didn't seem to offer much in the way of positive reflections on what I'd accomplished with my life thus far.

And I wouldn't even be able to watch those rom-coms or action movies on my own. I still had no TV, no DVD player. There was literally nothing in my apartment to watch or look at, aside from my cats.

AND WATCH MY CATS, I did. I watched them as they slept in their new beds, and as Homer—creeping along quietly and believing, as always, that "silent" and "invisible" were the same thing—attempted to annex Scarlett's bed the moment she got out of it, receiving an imperious slap of her front paw as his reward. I watched as all three of them began engaging in extraordinarily elaborate grooming rituals, attempting to combat the static electricity that made the job of ridding themselves of pesky bits of stray fur and dust far more onerous than it had been back in Miami. Their own shed fur clung to them, as did fur from the other cats. Strands of Vashti's white fur stuck to Homer's ebony coat—or vice versa—and Scarlett's gray tabby tufts, which occupied a sort of hued middle ground between them, were conspicuous on all three cats. And no matter how much I tried to clean (which wasn't too hard, since there wasn't any furniture), if there was a single speck of dust or strand of my own hair floating around, it seemed to find its way eventually to my cats' flanks and tails, held fast by a static-electric charge.

All the extra grooming forced my cats to roll onto their backs more than usual, to reach those hard-to-get spots, and of course all the extra rolling just made more static accumulate in their fur. I'd never thought much about how often or vigorously my cats groomed themselves—cats' grooming had, for some years now, simply been a part of the "background noise" of my everyday life, like the way you stop hearing the crashing of the tides when you live on a beach. But, with so little else to pay attention to—without the blare of the television or a constantly ringing phone to distract me—I noticed it now. I started noticing, or at least consciously thinking about, other things, too. Things I realized I'd known on some level all along, but had stopped paying attention to somewhere along the way.

I'd always felt that I knew the three of them well, of course. I was their "mom." Who could possibly know my cats better or more intimately than I did? I'd always thought of myself as a conscientious cat custodian, able to recite, at a moment's notice, complete personal and medical histories, food preferences, sleeping habits, and so on.

But, during our first two weeks in New York, I got to know them even better than I already had—and to wonder about things that I might have noticed before, but had never contemplated the meaning of. Scarlett, for example, always kicked her left hind leg twice when exiting the litter box. She was the most fastidious of all my cats, and hated tracking even a speck of litter outside of the box if she could help it. But, even if there weren't any obvious particles clinging to her fur when she exited, she still always did that little two-step kick before she considered her business concluded. Why? Was it merely a habit? Some sort of obsessive-compulsive ritual that she couldn't have rid herself of, even if she'd wanted to? Had some unwelcome tagalong from the litter box once stuck to her back paw in her younger days, irritating her for hours and leaving an indelible impression that persisted even all these years later? Or perhaps, I reflected, this was new behavior since our move to New York, some response to our new environment that made some kind of logical sense to Scarlett, even if its logic wasn't at all apparent to me.

Scarlett was also the least inherently trusting of my cats—and yet, she was the only one who ever slept sprawled out on her back, four white paws in the air with her white tummy exposed to whoever might happen by. To make herself so vulnerable when she slept—the time when she was already most vulnerable to begin with—seemed incongruous with what I knew of Scarlett's personality. It was a genuine puzzle, when I paused to give it some thought, and one that I still don't have an entirely satisfactory answer to—beyond noting that Scarlett had gained, by far, the most weight of any of them over the years, and at a certain point she was probably most comfortable simply letting it all hang loose, so to speak.

Vashti liked to sleep in a loaf-of-bread posture, on her belly with her head up and her four little paws tucked beneath her. And she never drank water directly from her water bowl—or from the bathtub faucet, which she occasionally pestered me about until I turned it on for her. Instead, she'd daintily dip a paw into the water and then, when it was thoroughly soaked, lick the droplets from her paw. It was a habit that I'd been dimly aware of, but had always thought of it as her "washing her hands." I tried now to remember if I'd ever seen her actually lapping water directly from a water source, and found that I couldn't recall a single instance of it. And wasn't that an odd thing to notice for the first time about a cat I'd been living with for nearly six years?

Every morning, and despite his blindness, Homer unerringly found, with the accuracy of a heat-seeking missile, the warm patch of sunlight that fell through our windows onto the floor at eight a.m. The pure coal black of his fur glowed a warm chocolatey brown in direct sunlight, with tabby stripes of a slightly darker brown, and how was it possible that I'd never realized before, or even thought about, how heart-stoppingly beautiful that was? Whenever he slept in the sun, he liked to fling one paw over the space where his eyes would have been—another thing I'd noticed but never really considered. It wasn't as if the brightness of the light falling across his face would have woken him up. Was it an instinctive response to the heat, the way the muscles around his sockets tightened, as if he were blinking, if a blast of air hit his face?

Homer, in some ways, fared better than the rest of us—not only because the darkness of our lamp-less apartment at night couldn't possibly matter to him, but also because I'd packed his beloved stuffed worm into his carrier with him when we'd flown from

Miami to New York. He, at least, had something well-loved and familiar to keep him company in this strange new place. I'd been cognizant enough of his love for that worm to think to pack it with him when we traveled, but I hadn't given it much consideration aside from, *Homer really likes that worm.* I thought now, though, what an odd thing it was that *this* bedraggled, slightly woebegone toy—of all the things I'd so lovingly set before Scarlett in the earliest days of her kitten-hood—had been the one and only store-bought toy that had stood the test of time, cherished by all three of my cats in their turn until it had finally fallen to Homer, who'd claimed it definitively as his own special property. As much as Scarlett and Vashti had enjoyed it before him, they'd never fallen asleep with it between their front paws, as Homer habitually did, one whiskered cheek resting peacefully atop it in the sunlight.

I'd toss a crumpled up piece of paper I'd filched from my new office for Scarlett and Vashti's entertainment (we had to have *something* to do to kill the time, after all), and remember what a very hard time Scarlett had given me with her resolute indifference to me, and to anything having to do with me, during our earliest days together, when she was still the first and only cat I'd ever lived with. For the past year or so, she'd come to cuddle up next to me on a fairly regular basis, and how was it possible that I'd forgotten to remember what an extraordinary turn of events that was? And Vashti's love of fetch! One night Vashti brought me a straight piece of paper that she'd nicked from the windowsill where (in lieu of a desk or a dresser or *anything at all* with drawers or shelves) I'd taken to storing work supplies, clearly intending that I should crumple and throw it for her, so she could retrieve it for me to throw again. Vashti hadn't been especially interested in fetch since she was a kitten—but, as a kitten, fetch had been a deep and abiding passion of hers. But I hadn't thought about that at all—hadn't even remembered it—in at least four years.

I noticed this, and a million other little things—the way Scarlett would always use her front right paw to spill three kibbles of dry food onto the floor, and then eat them from the ground, before dipping her head into the bowl to eat properly. The way Vashti would stand in a patch of sunlight, lift her head, and half-close her eyes for a moment, basking in the warmth, before ceding the sunny spot to Homer with remarkable good grace. The way Homer's tail would puff up slightly only at its base, whenever he vibrated it with the joy of encountering me upon our waking up first thing in the morning.

I realize that this all sounds like ridiculous minutiae—the inevitable result of a bored mind with far too little to occupy it. And, without question, it was. But I can also say with complete honesty that I likely would never have become a cat writer, some seven or eight years later, if not for this period of enforced reveries, during which I got to know my cats from scratch, all over again.

KEEP IN MIND THAT this was only a two-week period that I'm writing about. If it seems longer in my memory now, or in the retelling, it's probably because the swiftness and entirety of the change between my old life—loaded with friends, beach days, and a cheerful, cluttered apartment—and this new, decidedly emptier, one couldn't have been a greater shock. And I have to think all the way back to my go-round with chicken pox in my early twenties (yikes) to recall a more physically uncomfortable two weeks I've ever experienced. There were days when I honestly worried that

I might be developing a hunch, or encouraging some other sort of incipient spinal deformity, from sleeping on that ever-deflating mattress that offered essentially nothing in the way of cushion between my back and the floor. By the time Valentine's Day finally rolled around, I didn't need to worry about feeling sorry for myself while looking at all the bouquets and stuffed teddy bears, holding little stuffed hearts, on my female coworkers' desks. It was literally impossible for me to turn my neck in any direction, so many pinched nerves did I have. I could focus only on the computer screen and work directly in front of me on my own desk—which, I suppose, was good for my productivity, if not for my state of mind.

Every moment when the cats actually seemed happy in their new home, I counted as a triumph. Every moment when they seemed unhappy or uncomfortable, I asked myself whether I had, in fact, ruined their lives—which of course naturally made me wonder if I'd managed to ruin my own as well. Of all the things I'd thought about when contemplating this move, static electricity hadn't even been among them—and yet, the dry and hyper-charged air of our new home was probably the most disconcerting thing for all of us. I couldn't seem to avoid shocking myself on doorknobs or the stovetop. And my cats simply couldn't understand why touching things—which was, after all, an unavoidable part of everyday life—suddenly meant enduring a tiny, but still startling, twinge of pain. It happened when they touched me, or each other, or brushed up against the metal handle of a kitchen cabinet. And how could they even escape the occasional encounter with a kitchen cabinet, or the hinge of a closet or bathroom door, when there was no furniture for them to rest on or hide under? The lack of anything to perch on—of a comfortable sofa or bed, long-since made their own with scratches and scent marking—was deeply

unsettling in and of itself. The heated cat beds made things somewhat easier for all of us. Still, none of us were feeling particularly
jazzed about this alarming and seemingly merit-less life change I'd
foisted upon us all.

And then, just like that, everything changed.

A couple of days before Valentine's Day, it finally snowed. It
wasn't the first time I'd ever seen snow, but—unless you counted
a couple of very light dustings while I was in college in Atlanta—it
was the first time I'd seen snow in any significant quantities since
I was sixteen years old, when a high-school class trip had brought
me to Boston in the winter.

Eventually, the snow that had fallen to cover the streets and
sidewalks of New York City would turn yellow from dog-walkers
and black from muddy boots and car tires, before being shoved
into mounds on street corners and hardening into ice piles that
made the simple act of crossing on foot at an intersection a difficult
endeavor, at best. But, for that first day or two, it was beautiful. It
was glorious. It's hard to explain the sheer wonder that a trans-
planted Miamian feels upon seeing a city like New York blanketed
in snow for the first time. The endless, perfect whiteness of it,
stretching for miles and miles when viewed from the windows of a
high-rise apartment building—the hush that falls over the city, the
way that all its hard edges are softened and blurred. The slate-gray
of the sky before the snow had turned the entire city the same
dulled gray. Now though, for just a day or two, its streets and
buildings glowed gently with a kind of pearlescent aura, casting
a bright gleam onto the faces of the handful of pedestrians hardy
enough to traverse the sidewalks while the snow was still falling,
before shovels and snowplows had done their job.

Watching through my windows as the snow fell, in my corner
apartment way up on the thirty-first floor, was like being inside a

snow globe. Scarlett and Vashti were as enchanted with it as I was. Scarlett climbed to a windowsill and, standing up on her hind legs like a prairie dog, batted her paw gently again and again at the panes of glass, trying to catch the flakes that danced tantalizingly just beyond her reach. She stretched her neck and craned her head to see as far upward as she could, clearly filled with as much wide-eyed wonder as I was as she took in a spectacle that not only hadn't she ever seen before, but had never even known might exist. She sat there for hours with her head turned up and her front paws pressed against the glass, only occasionally looking back over her shoulder at the rest of us. *Does everybody else see this?* she seemed to be asking. *What* is *all this wonderful white stuff?!*

As for Vashti, my arctic fox of a cat, something deep and instinctive within her seemed to recognize the snow instantly. I had my reservations about letting Scarlett and Vashti out onto the small balcony of my apartment (that Homer would *never* go out on that balcony, of course, went without saying). But Vashti ran back and forth between me and the balcony door so anxiously, and with such plaintive squeaks of entreaty, that I couldn't resist her. I put on my old bomber jacket and a pair of rubber galoshes (the closest thing I had to snow boots that winter) and stood shivering on the balcony with her as she plunged deep into the highest drift where the wind had blown the snow against one balcony wall. She leapt and burrowed and tunneled into the snow, the whiteness of her fur disappearing into it so completely that eventually she was only discernible by the contrast her emerald-green eyes and little pink nose made against the white-on-white landscape she created. She wasn't as happy when, upon our reentry indoors, I bundled her up and rubbed her down vigorously with a towel. But then I stepped into the shower myself, turning on the hot water at full blast, and

Vashti dozed contentedly atop the clothes hamper in the steamy bathroom, as drowsily contented as an old man taking a *shvitz*.

Homer couldn't see the snow, and so didn't quite understand what all the fuss was about. But the sound of the cold wind outside was stilled for once, muffled by the falling snow, and the rest of us seemed unusually contented—and the ever-empathic Homer picked up on our mood, and was contented himself. I made some instant cocoa in the microwave and poured it into one of the Styrofoam cups I'd been accumulating in my small kitchen until my dishes and glassware finally arrived, then inflated my air mattress and sat, with my cocoa beside me, propped up on my pillows against the wall. Homer climbed into my lap, then burrowed his way beneath the ancient sweatshirt I wore until his small head popped out through the neck—which I'd cut and widened back in my college days (as early-90s fashion had dictated). I gently rubbed Homer's head with one hand, and turned the pages of a book with the other and, for the two or three hours before the air mattress deflated once again, I reveled in the deep warmth of his purr against my chest and neck while the snow fell silently outside. Scarlett and Vashti, having exhausted themselves, slept soundly in their heated cat beds.

Despite having wanted, for almost as long as I could remember, to move to New York, I'd been homesick beyond the telling of it for the past two weeks. "Home," in my mind, still meant Miami. Miami was warm and familiar and easy, whereas everything about New York so far had proven to be cold and strange and just *hard*. I had been embarrassed to admit it to myself, and had never once mentioned the homesickness that churned in the pit of my stomach, night and day, to the family and friends I'd left behind—some of whom, at my going-away party, had predicted that I'd be back within a few months. *Not me,* I'd assured them. *Never.* Faced with the reality of actually living here, though, my certainty had wavered considerably. Still, I was stubborn and proud and felt that I'd rather let myself be drawn and quartered than acknowledge that maybe the naysayers had been right, and that moving to Manhattan had been a colossal mistake.

Now, though—for once—everything here was white and quiet and peaceful and warm. Scarlett, on her back in her little cat bed with all four paws in the air, snored lightly in her sleep. Vashti had positioned herself in her own bed so that she could see the snow on the balcony when she half-opened her eyes from time to time, already imagining further adventures whenever I consented to go out there with her again. But I was in no hurry. The warm weight of Homer lying against my chest beneath my shirt dispelled that ever-present knot of homesickness in the pit of my stomach. I paused in my reading to marvel at the feeling of it being gone, and dropped a kiss on the top of Homer's head.

"You're my good boy," I murmured into his black fur. "You're my good, good boy." And Homer, as warm and contented for the moment as I was, lifted his chin to nuzzle his head into my neck, purring harder.

AFTER THAT, IT WAS as if a fever had broken—a strange, cold sort of fever, to be sure.

The apartment was still chilly and mostly empty, and it didn't take long for the snow outside to turn into an irritating and unappealing slush that even Vashti lost interest in. But the feeling engendered by the moment of grace that had descended on all of us the day it snowed lingered. Whatever feelings of guilt (on my part), of resentment (on the cats' part), or homesickness (on all our parts) had evaporated the way the last traces of that snow eventually would within a few weeks.

It was only two days later—on Valentine's Day, as fate would have it—when my furniture and belongings were finally delivered. Out from the moving van and into my apartment came our bed, our couch, our coffee table, our rugs, our lamps, our plates and silverware and assorted knickknacks. The apartment felt smaller once it was filled, but also infinitely more comfortable. The smell of new paint and varnish gave way to the familiar scent of us, and the life we'd made together over the years.

The best Valentine's Day gift I could have asked for—better than a box of candy or a dozen red roses to display on the desk of my office—was the deep and comfortable sleep I enjoyed that first night when I finally had my own bed back. If I'd had anyone to invite, I might actually have thrown a party to celebrate ditching that wretched air mattress in my building's trash room.

I didn't have anybody who I could have invited to a party then, but eventually I would. Eventually the weather would turn warmer, and I'd befriend coworkers and colleagues. And in August of that year, at the rooftop birthday party for a friend of a friend, I'd end up meeting a hilarious film journalist named Laurence. I didn't even suspect, that first night, that I would end up marrying him someday. But I did know, from the very first time we spoke, that he was the funniest person I'd ever met, and that I wanted to spend as much time with him as I could decently get away with. (He had a girlfriend back then, who I also met that night—but that's a story for another time.)

Things got better, in other words. And I never did end up moving back to Miami, despite some of the pessimistic predictions that certain friends of mine—and that I, myself, in moments of despair—had made.

But before any of that happened, even before the furniture arrived, I'd gotten over the unsettling feeling of homesickness and constant strangeness in this new place. Yes, my new life in New York was new and different, frequently cold and, for a brief time, empty of the familiar things I'd collected over the years. Yet, even still, I realized, I was luckier than most people.

"Home," to me, had never meant a precise place or city or collection of rooms. It wasn't a certain smell or type of climate or a specific piece of furniture.

For me, home was wherever my cats were. And my cats would always come with me, wherever I went. We'd never been the exiles, the vagabonds cast onto the strange shores of a cold and unfamiliar place, that in darker moments I'd imagined us to be.

It had been foolish, I realized, ever to have felt homesick. The four of us had never left our home. We'd been home the whole time.

Spray Anything

It's difficult to rouse Clayton—a cheerful, affectionate mush of a cat—into anything approaching anger, and if you were trying to pick a fight with him on purpose you'd probably find yourself stumped. You could yank away a beloved toy he was playing with, pull a half-chewed cat treat right out of his mouth, shove him unceremoniously off your own or someone else's lap, stroke his fur the wrong way for a solid half-hour (as our young nephew did on one occasion), stick him full of needles like they do at the vet's office, where Clayton is beloved—and all you'd get for your trouble would be purrs and head-bonks and a series of "MEEEEEEE"s entreating your friendship as he happily hippi-ty-hopped after you on his three good legs. "Clayton's a stuffed animal," I'm fond of saying, and with his ultra-soft, velvet-plush black belly, he does bear a strong resemblance to the Gund teddy bears I was so fond of as a child. Nothing, in other words, could be less threatening than Clayton.

Even the proximity of unknown cats—a universally reliable instigator of feline hostility—tends not to rile Clayton. Neighborhood and feral cats make fairly frequent pit stops in our tiny backyard, and Clayton, from his post by the French doors leading from our kitchen out to the yard, generally takes in this sight with unruffled equanimity. He isn't fazed in the slightest even when these strange cats—upon catching a glimpse of Clayton sitting on his one haunch and observing them with friendly interest—arch their backs and puff up their tails, unsure what to make of the little black oddball who apparently never got the memo that cats are supposed to be wary of other cats they don't know. A few years back, a feral mama cat gave birth in the space between the wooden fences separating our yard from our next-door neighbor's. Far from being irritated at seeing a portion of his territory commandeered in this way, Clayton appeared ready—if not delighted—to welcome this feline family with open paws. The spectacle of two fuzzy kittens gamboling among our trees and shrubs proved an especially frustrating allure. Whenever one of the kittens wandered close to the house, Clayton would stretch all the way up against the French doors on his one hind leg—front paws pressed eagerly against the glass panes—or else promptly roll onto his back to expose his tummy and look at me pleadingly with big yellow eyes that eloquently begged, *Please, pleeeeeeeeease let me play with those kittens!*

Eventually, when the kittens were old enough to be weaned but still young enough to be socialized, we trapped the whole family with the assistance of our local TNR (trap-neuter-return) group, Neighborhood Cats, so the mama could be spayed and the kittens adopted out into permanent homes. It was the happiest possible ending—and certainly the most responsible one—but, still, it was a sad day for all of us when we saw the last of the kittens. Clayton especially.

Just about the only sure way of getting Clayton's dander up is when a transient feline puts our backyard to use for . . . let's say "darker" deeds. For a good month or so, the cat who lives three doors down took to dropping into our yard a few times each week to poop in the patch of grass beneath our stone bench. He always seemed to stop by when Clayton happened to be making his daily backdoor rounds, and Clayton's all-pupil eyes would pop so far out of his head with rage (the neighbor cat's own eyes half-closed in an expression of deep and peaceful contemplation as he did his business) that I worried Clayton might actually be on the verge of an aneurism.

Fanny is generally a much cooler customer than Clayton. She doesn't deign to notice such things as *who* in the neighborhood is pooping *where*, nor does it seem to bother her if an errant feline visitor pauses long enough in his travels to give a territorial urine spray to our fence and rosebushes. (Although it should be noted that Fanny herself routinely sprays up the side of her litter box, rather than crouching to relieve herself in a more ladylike fashion, which perhaps makes her more sympathetic to spraying by others.)

Clayton, on the other hand, is invariably incensed. His ears stretch and flatten out to the sides until the top of his head is perfectly horizontal, and—squeaking his indignation as loudly as he's able (having never really mastered a mature cat's full-throated meow)—he'll take a few steps forward and backward, then forward and backward again, his whole little body quivering in outrage as he turns up a look at me that says, *Do you see this?! DO YOU SEE WHAT THAT CAT IS DOING TO OUR ROSES???!!!*

It was Clayton's consternation that first drew my attention to the new guy—a big bruiser of a tuxedo cat—who showed up in our yard one August day, about a month ago, to spray our bushes and startle the birds from our trees. Generally, those of us inside the house take far more notice of the outside cats than they do of us. To the extent that any of them regard Clayton at all, it's either with the aforementioned arched-back, tail-up wary hostility, or else with the sort of disdainful indifference that you might expect a rough-and-tumble outdoor cat to reserve for a pudgy, squeaky-voiced mama's boy who spends an absurd percentage of his day being hand-fed treats while curled up on a soft pillow in his human's lap.

And, at first, this encounter seemed to follow the regular pattern. It was a sunny weekday afternoon, and Clayton mightily mew-squeaked his ire over the invading tuxie while I rinsed out the cats' food bowls preparatory to serving them lunch. The cat outside, having given our rosebushes a thorough hosing, lazily strolled about the yard. It wasn't until Fanny joined us in the kitchen, as she always does upon hearing the scraping and rinsing of bowls that means lunch is imminent, when the pattern long established by so many visits from other cats was disrupted.

I knew from experience how nearly impossible it was to hear anything through the French doors when they were securely closed. From the tuxedo cat's perspective, Clayton must have appeared more than a little ridiculous—a hopping-mad three-legged cat, doing a little back-and-forth stomping "dance" while his pink mouth opened and closed in unheard protest. Fanny had joined Clayton before the French doors, sitting on her haunches and delicately curling her long, sinuous black tail around the dainty little feet that always provided such a contrast next to Clayton's wider pads. Unlike Clayton, who was completely caught up in policing the tuxedo cat's crimes and misdemeanors against our backyard flora, Fanny's head was down, her attention absorbed by a little feathered mouse toy that she batted around idly with one front paw.

The tuxedo cat's yellow eyes had raked over Clayton once or twice in apparent boredom as he raised his nose into the air, eyelids partially lowered against the sun, to take a few exploratory sniffs of the air in this unfamiliar terrain. But when the cat caught sight of Fanny, his eyes flew open and his entire body froze. And then something happened that had never happened even once in all the through-the-windows encounters we'd had with outdoor cats over the years.

His eyes firmly fixed on Fanny, the tuxedo cat began walking forward—with a slow, deliberate step—straight over to where my cats were sitting on the other side of the French doors.

Fanny appeared oblivious to this development. Clayton, for the first time in all his puffed-up scoldings of backyard cats, seemed uncertain. His back-and-forth stomping ceased, and he took a single, decisive step backward, the fur on his back rising slightly in alarm. It was one thing, after all, to yell your head off at someone twice your size who was completely ignoring you—but quite another when that twice-your-size someone was headed right *for* you, with every apparent intention of taking you up on the confrontation you'd implied with all your yelling.

In a sense, all the time we'd spent over the years watching the cats who visited our backyard had felt almost like a play or a movie—a one-way viewing experience, in other words. We observed the feline "performers," but they took little or no notice of us. The French doors through which we observed them served as a sort of "fourth wall" that—except for occasional eye contact or momentary wariness—was never broken. Even those backyard kittens Clayton had wanted so desperately to play with, for all his cajoling and clowning attempts to get their attention, had never given any indication of being aware of his presence. So to have this new cat not only see and acknowledge us, but start walking right over *to* us, was unnerving—like being in a comedy club and heckling a comedian who not only heckles you back, but actually steps down from the stage and into the audience, heading your way to confront you physically and directly.

I had just gotten a can of cat food out of the cabinet and, holding it along with the cats' freshly cleaned bowls, I moved instinctively to stand behind Clayton and Fanny. I knew, of course, that they were entirely safe behind the closed and locked kitchen doors. I wasn't sure, however, that Clayton himself was aware of this. I couldn't tell if the shiver that ran from his shoulders through the tip of his thick tail was heightened anger or the beginnings of fear. The thought of Clayton being afraid in his own home was an upsetting one, to say the least, and my first impulse was to make a loud noise and big, sudden movements, for the sake of frightening this strange tuxedo cat away.

But I hesitated. It's probably not an exaggeration to say that I'd never once in my whole life frightened a cat on purpose, and I found myself reluctant to do so now, especially since my own cats weren't in any actual danger.

For her part, Fanny's attention remained rapt on the mouse toy at her feet, which she continued to bat around in a desultory way with her left paw, unaware of the drama unfolding around her. It wasn't until the tuxedo cat was so close to the doors that his pink nose was almost pressed against the glass that she finally looked up, directly into his face.

Everything went still. Even Clayton seemed to hold his breath—as did I—though his gaze swung wildly back and forth between his sister's face and that of the interloper. The two cats' eyes locked for a long, unblinking moment, and I—a hopelessly ignorant human observer to this bit of inscrutable feline byplay—wasn't sure what to make of their expressions. Tension formed a knot in my stomach as I waited for the outside cat to snarl or throw his body against the glass or do something else overtly aggressive.

But the tension of the moment was broken suddenly as the tuxedo cat, finally, blinked once or twice—which, in cat language, is an unmistakably sociable signal. In the manner of a puppy, he cocked his head to one side at a pleasant, curious angle. He brought one front paw up into the air and tapped gently a few times at the glass right in front of Fanny's face. *Hello. Are you friendly?*

Fanny blinked back at the cat, but all four of her own paws remained firmly on the ground. She rose from her haunches and arched her back ever so slightly—not with an air of aggression, as Clayton had earlier, but more as if she were simply stretching her muscles a bit after having been sitting down. She didn't acknowledge the tuxedo cat's rap against the glass with any return gesture. Instead, turning her head to where I remained standing—clean bowls still in one hand and a can of cat food in the other—she turned her back to the outside cat and walked over to the spot on the floor near the kitchen counter where I usually serve the cats' meals.

The tuxedo cat lingered at the door for a moment, watching Fanny's retreat into the shadowy recesses of the kitchen with large, unblinking eyes. Then, casting an indifferent look at the now-silent Clayton, he also turned his back. Crossing the yard, the tuxedo cat leapt nimbly onto a tree branch. With one last glance back into our kitchen, he disappeared over the fence and was gone.

I GOT TO KNOW the cat well, at least by sight, over the next few days. He was taller than either Clayton or Fanny, and broader. In contrast with Clayton's soft plumpness, his was the stockiness of muscle, the shifting weight of which, as he strode around our yard, added an inevitable swagger to his feline prowl. His tuxedo markings were so nearly perfect that it was almost as if someone had started with an all-white cat and then painted a cat-size tuxedo onto him. He had a black mask over his ears and eyes and the top of his nose, and from the bridge of his nose down his face was entirely white, which made it look as if he were dressed for a masked ball. His breastbone featured two sideways triangles of white surrounded by black, like the collar of a tuxedo shirt peeping over a tuxedo jacket, and the pattern continued down his mostly white chest, also flanked by black "lapels." (All he was missing to perfect the look was a little red boutonniere pinned to his chest.) He had a black back and tail, a white belly, and predominantly black legs, with four little white "socks."

He rolled onto his back one day while lounging on a sunny patch of the brick tile surrounding our backyard grill, and a quick glance confirmed that he was not only male, but extravagantly male—which is to say, he hadn't been neutered. This led me to believe that he was a true feral and not simply a runaway house-cat—an impression corroborated by the rakish way his left ear flopped over, which I thought might be a souvenir from some long-ago tussle with another cat. The floppy ear, as contrasted with the stiff formality of his tuxedo markings, gave the cat a slightly gone-to-seed air—like a down-at-heel lounge singer at four a.m., collar undone and bow tie unknotted, pounding whiskey shots at a dive bar following a late-night set.

There have always been women who go for that kind of thing, women who know that George Clooney in the role of Danny Ocean is infinitely more attractive walking out the prison gates with an undone tux and five o'clock shadow than he would've been if he were immaculate. There are women who see a man who looks brooding, dark, dangerous, untamed—a man who looks as if he'd be just as apt to filch money out of your wallet as spend his own money on you—and think, *That's for me.* The pull that "bad boys" exert on the sheltered daughters of respectable, middle-class homes is, after all, as old as the telling of love stories.

It's possible—I don't say *definite*, mind you, I only say *possible*—that I may have known a thing or two about that myself, back in my own younger days. (Ahem.)

But Fanny, at least initially, was emphatically not her mother's daughter in this regard. After their first encounter through the glass, it was as if the tuxedo cat had turned invisible as far as Fanny was concerned. He started coming around every afternoon at one o'clock—the time when I gave the cats their lunch, and when Fanny was thus guaranteed to be present in the kitchen—and Fanny couldn't have been less interested. He'd strut around the yard impressively for a minute or two, vigorously spray our back fence a few times, and then, with a sort of studied nonchalance, drift closer to our French doors. Whenever Fanny walked near enough to be visible through the shadows cast inside by the bright sunlight outside, he'd tap one front paw gently against the glass. She'd pause midstride and send a brief, uninterested glance over her shoulder at the cat (*Oh . . . you again?*), then continue on her way.

It was a thoroughly perplexing dynamic, one that I contemplated more than I should have as three or four more days went by, and the pattern was repeated as precisely, each afternoon, as if it were a prearranged and choreographed routine. It was one thing for two cats to overcome their initial wariness and become friends. But I racked my brain trying to remember a single time I'd ever heard of two cats deciding to become friends *at first sight*. And while I wasn't entirely sure that Fanny herself had decided on anything—it actually seemed as if the only decision she'd made was to decide nothing at all—there was no mistaking the admiration in the tuxedo cat's eyes as he stared after her (or the aggressively territorial way in which he sprayed our bushes every day, to the point that no other cat now dared enter our yard). It seemed clear that, for his part, our backyard tom intended to stake some sort of claim on our home and its occupants. Or, at least, *one* of its occupants.

Sadly for the backyard tuxie, however, of our two cats, the only one whose attention he had definitively captured was Clayton. Clayton was beside himself these days. I'd never thought that anything could distract his attention from the preparation of his meals, but that was before Clayton became obsessed with our constant gardener and his daily ministrations to our backyard foliage. Clayton would stomp and squeak and kick up an awful fuss—at least until the outside cat approached the doors, at which point Clayton would dart behind my legs or deeper into the kitchen, sometimes all the way to the opposite wall and the door that led out to the front of our house. "Mommy's little chicken hawk," I took to calling him.

Once or twice, when I was close enough to Clayton to make him feel that he had backup, he tried standing his ground directly in front of the backyard cat, who, by the time he got close to the French doors, was always craning his neck around, trying to catch a glimpse of Fanny. With Clayton standing before him, the outdoor cat would pull his lips back in a hiss—not so much an aggressive hiss, as if he were preparing to attack, but more like a hiss of irritation that Clayton was blocking his view inside. *Get out of the way, man . . . I'm trying to eyeball your sister.*

If Clayton didn't like the strange cat's interest in our rosebushes, he was even *less* enthusiastic about the strange cat's interest in his sister.

After a few days of getting no response from Fanny whatsoever, the backyard tuxie resorted to a cat's tried-and-true method of getting attention: He began knocking things over. Little flower-pots and ceramic knickknacks and candleholders that we'd stud-ded throughout our postage-stamp backyard were sent mercilessly crashing to the ground from their perches on wooden shelves or the wrought-iron table where we occasionally enjoyed a meal al fresco. On the one hand, I couldn't bring myself to mourn the loss of our potted plants, as it saved me the daily trouble of having to water the wretched things. (How I missed living in Manhattan, where sidewalk trees either grew or didn't grow, with no input from me!) On the other hand, having to clean up shards of shat-tered clay flowerpots and spilled soil and the broken remnants of various and sundry other tchotchkes (some of which I actually *did* like) wasn't exactly an enjoyable replacement chore.

This stratagem on the tuxedo cat's part met with only limited success. Coincidentally or by design (and, for the life of me, I wasn't sure which), Fanny had started spending more time in the kitchen, napping for hours atop the kitchen island or on a sunlit patch of tile before the French doors. And she would, indeed, look up with mild alarm whenever she heard the crash of something or other going over in the backyard. But after a brief, startled look around the kitchen confirmed that there was nothing—nothing *inside*, at any rate—that was worth her attention, her eyes would close or turn away. Even Clayton, who didn't seem particularly interested in what the cat was doing when he wasn't defiling our rosebushes, wasn't impressed by these antics.

The tuxedo cat may have disdained to treat poor Clayton as if he were any kind of credible threat, but he was warier of Laurence and me, turning tail and climbing up the rose trellis and over the stone wall that separates our garden from the one belonging to the house behind ours whenever we went out into the backyard. Laurence caught sight of his retreating black tail one evening (the tuxedo cat's daily visits by now having extended into all-day hang-arounds) when we went out to grill some turkey burgers for dinner.

"Was that a cat?" Laurence asked—having only moments earlier noted our sudden lack of potted flowers and the "skunky smell" that now permeated our garden.

"That's Fanny's boyfriend, Bruiser," I replied matter-of-factly. I'd taken to calling the cat Bruiser in my mind, and it seemed an appropriate name—although I should have been more careful about that. Naming anything is always the first step in claiming an ownership stake.

It was inevitable that I would begin to feel a vested interest in any cat—apparently belonging to nobody—who showed up in our yard day after day. The feeling that somehow—maybe?—this cat was meant to be *our* cat was growing as the days passed, even as I worried about this mysterious new presence in our lives. Just what *was* this cat's interest in Fanny, anyway? Having been spayed as a very young kitten, before we'd even adopted her, Fanny was in no position to give Bruiser any little Bruisers. Surely Bruiser himself was instinctively aware of this. So what *was* it about Fanny that he found so compelling?

And there was an even more worrisome thought: What if Fanny decided to return the stray cat's affections at some point? The conventional wisdom among cat experts is that no cat is ever fully domesticated. And I knew that this—the sense of living with a semi-wild and ultimately unknowable creature—is the secret fascination cats hold for many of us who love them deeply. It might seem paradoxical to love something because it can never be entirely tamed and then—because you love it so much—set out to do exactly that. And yet, what could be a greater joy than earning the love of someone who didn't *need* to love anybody but nevertheless *chose* to love you? When you got right down to it, wasn't that the real allure of the "bad boy" himself?

It had always seemed to me that no creature could be less "untamable" or "unknowable" than Clayton. It was hard to imagine anybody being *more* transparent or human-dependent. But Fanny—with her solitary habits and endless (and endlessly frustrated) craving for the hunt—perpetually seemed to hang just slightly beyond our reach. It had occurred to me that maybe the reason Bruiser had latched on to Fanny so quickly was because he understood her in some deep-down way that I would never be able to.

"Oh," Laurence replied as he began laying out turkey burgers, then turned back to me with a puzzled expression. "Fanny's *what*?"

"Well, I don't know if I'd call him her 'boyfriend,' exactly." I began arranging plates and condiments on the little wrought-iron backyard table. "It's more like he's her *admirer*, maybe? Anyway, he's definitely wooing her."

"You've lost your mind," Laurence informed me.

"It's true!" I insisted. "He comes here every single day just to look at her through the windows. It's very sweet." I paused to nibble nonchalantly on a pickle spear, then added, "I think I may start putting out food for him."

"Oh, no you don't." Laurence closed the lid of the grill and turned to face me. "We are *not* getting a third cat."

I spread my hands wide in a gesture of innocence. "Who said anything about getting a third cat?"

"Like I don't know how you think," Laurence said. "First you'll say this cat has 'chosen' us . . ."

"Which he really kind of has," I interjected.

"And then you'll say that we have to take responsibility for him," Laurence continued.

"Which we *do*," I said firmly. "At the very least, if we can trap him and get him neutered, then we have to. We can't just let him run around making more stray kittens."

Laurence turned to raise the lid of the grill and flip the turkey burgers, saying over his shoulder, "And *that* is how we end up with a third cat."

"Look," I said reasonably. "I don't even know if this is a cat who can be socialized to live with people. And Clayton *hates* him, which obviously has to factor into any long-term decisions. But if he's going to spend so much time here, then we need to make sure he's getting food . . ."

"Which will only make him spend *more* time here," Laurence said.

"*And*," I continued, "we need to take him to the vet and get him fixed and make sure he gets his shots. You don't want Fanny's boyfriend to be some rabid stray, do you?"

"I don't see why Fanny needs a boyfriend at all," Laurence grumbled.

I looked for a moment at Fanny and Clayton, watching us from the kitchen in eager anticipation of bits of turkey burger—a reliable grilling-season treat—and I remembered my own youth, when the long, long days of July and August had seemed to hold an endless, if undefined, promise.

"Everybody wants a summer romance," I said.

FANNY WAS A BIG believer in presents—every single night, for at least the last five years, she had thoughtfully left one of her own favorite toys (or sometimes something less adorable, like a roach carcass) on Laurence's and my pillows before bedtime. The giving of gifts was a gesture that clearly had a deep and resonant meaning for Fanny, so I think it was Bruiser's presents that finally won her over—the presents themselves, or possibly the abject adoration, reminiscent of Lloyd Dobler in *Say Anything*, that was behind them. If Bruiser'd had a boom box and opposable thumbs, I have no doubt that he would have stood in our backyard holding that boom box over his head all day—or however long it took for Fanny to notice him.

Say Anything isn't precisely the correct point of reference, however—unless there's a blood-and-guts carnage scene in there that I missed. And I should probably put the word "gifts" in scare quotes, because Bruiser's offerings had nothing to do with romantic Peter Gabriel ballads and were decidedly more . . . well . . . yikes.

Coming downstairs into the darkened kitchen at five a.m. to feed the cats the next morning, I was confronted in the shadowy predawn by two glowing yellow eyes outside the back kitchen doors. In and of itself, this wouldn't have rattled me too much. But just below those luminescent eyes—appearing to float in a ghostly, disembodied way through the murky light—a large, bloodied, and distinctly dead rat was pressed up against the glass.

I felt my legs go liquid and cried out, loudly enough that it startled Clayton and Fanny—who'd been following closely behind me for the dispensing of their morning feast—right back up the stairs. Flipping on the kitchen lights both dulled the visibility of the rat and brought into focus the shadowy shape of Bruiser, who was clutching the rat in his mouth. Fanny was the first one of the cats who was brave enough to creep cautiously back downstairs, and she made a thorough inspection of the kitchen, nose to the ground as she surveilled every inch of the room for potential hazards while I spoke to her in a soothing voice, trying to reassure her that, despite my embarrassingly girly shriek of a moment ago, everything was perfectly safe.

It was still dark outside, which meant that Fanny had to get right up to the glass of the French doors before she could see through their mirrored reflections of the kitchen and make out anything beyond blurred shapes in the yard outside. Once she came face to face with Bruiser on the other side of the glass, he promptly dropped the rat and nosed it as close to the door—and Fanny's feet on the other side of it—as possible. Then, as he had the first time he saw her (and every day since), he brought one front paw up to the glass pane before her face and tapped at it gently.

The two of them sat there on their haunches in identical poses, staring at each other for a long moment and blinking occasionally. And then, for the first time, Fanny raised her own front paw and tapped the glass back at Bruiser. Bruiser paused in his tapping and simply held his paw to the glass, and for a moment it almost looked as if the two of them were touching their front paws together—Fanny's black with black "beans," Bruiser's white with pink "beans"—through the window that separated them.

Clayton's general feeling of outrage where Bruiser was concerned seemed tempered during this predawn reverie, when Bruiser wasn't graffiti-ing our yard with his spray. Clayton was, however, impatient for his breakfast, and his loud "*MEEEEEEEE!*"—accompanied by a coaxing nip at my ankle—tore me away from the romantic scene unfolding at the French doors. The sound of the lid being pulled from a can of cat food drew Fanny's attention as well, and with nary a backward glance she trotted over to the paw-print plastic mat where I set out the cats' food, and stood patiently next to Clayton while I dispensed their morning meal.

"It's all well and good for *you*," I observed, as she picked delicately at her breakfast with an unmistakably complacent air and Clayton wolfed his down beside her. "But I'm the one who has to figure out how to get rid of a rat corpse." And, sighing as I dug out thick rubber gloves, a plastic trash bag, and a shovel from the utility closet, I prepared to do just that. Bruiser headed for the back wall of the garden as soon as I turned the door handle, melting into the cool gray light of early morning.

I had no immediate inkling as to where, exactly, would be the appropriate place to dispose of rodent remains. (Once again I thought longingly of Manhattan apartment life, with its handy and ubiquitous trash chutes that you could just shove things into and then forget about them.) I finally settled on the dumpster behind Key Foods, three blocks away—reasoning that, among all the meat and produce they disposed of daily, one little (giant) rat wouldn't be noticed.

I set off as soon as I had Bruiser's "gift" bagged and sealed—not wanting to spend the next several hours thinking about it waiting for me in the backyard—and must have startled more than a few early-morning joggers and dog-walking neighbors: a bed-headed woman in pajama pants, an old T-shirt, and the sparkly kitten-heeled mules that had been closest to the front door, still wearing rubber gloves and carrying a trash bag and alternating between muttering under her breath and shuddering in disgust as she stalked the streets of Downtown Jersey City at five-thirty in the morning.

Seemingly encouraged by the first sign of genuine interest that Fanny had shown, Bruiser continued to deliver presents over the next several days. Mornings always saw a dead rat or a "bouquet" of mice gracing our back doorstep, and it was somewhat alarming to realize just how many rodents there apparently were in the general vicinity of our home. But Bruiser's gifts weren't restricted to the mornings, nor were they limited to rats and mice.

In the afternoons and early evenings, I would find things that had clearly come from our neighbors' trash cans, or possibly even from inside their homes (courtesy of unattended back porches or open windows): little piles of half-eaten spare ribs and Chinese takeout containers; crumpled aluminum tins that had once held pies; empty cans of tuna and cat food; holey socks and a frayed red bra (which seemed too *Showgirls*-esque to belong to any of our rather staid neighbors); pieces of costume jewelry and sparkly things that had fallen off children's toys; a plastic baggie of a green-ish-brown weed that turned out to be catnip, which was a relief as it spared me the potential awkwardness of having to go door to door asking our neighbors, *So . . . um . . . is this your marijuana?* Accompanying the catnip was a battered DVD case containing *The Sopornos 3*, which immediately raised two questions: First, just what exactly did Bruiser have in mind??? And second, what were Laurence and I supposed to do with *The Sopornos 3* when we hadn't even seen *The Sopornos 1* or *2*? (It's just so hard these days to start in the middle of a franchise.) Someone in our neighborhood clearly had a secret fetish for Twinkies, and someone else had a passion for menthol cigarettes and turkey jerky, judging from the number of only-half-consumed packs of both that began accumulating in our backyard. And while, as a writer, I'll admit to always having found it intriguing to get little glimpses into the hidden lives of others, petty theft isn't generally my preferred method of doing so.

I was also starting to feel a smidgen of guilt over having turned the Key Foods dumpster into a rodent graveyard.

Laurence and I wavered between amazement and dismay—amazement at Bruiser's sheer tenacity and ingenuity, and dismay at both the gifts themselves and also the clouds of flies that now routinely swarmed around our back doors at the site of his offerings. Frequently the flies made it inside the house when I opened those doors to dispose of whatever Bruiser had left, buzzing frantically through the kitchen and around our heads. This delighted Clayton and Fanny to no end (*I'm gonna EAT those flies!*), although my own personal—and perhaps uncharitable—opinion was that the price of their entertainment may have been too dear.

Still, we couldn't help but admire Bruiser's commitment. Even Laurence began to waver in his heretofore firmly held position that there would be no third cat added to our family. We were long past wondering whether or not Bruiser had, indeed, chosen us. That he had was now an accepted fact of our lives.

I'd started putting out a little paper plate of food for Bruiser in the backyard the afternoon of the morning when he'd brought the first rat. Even if the gifts were only for Fanny and not intended for the rest of us, the fact that he was bringing them at all—added to his now-constant presence in our backyard—meant in a hard-to-pin-down yet also indisputable way that he was now officially our cat. One of the implications of deciding he was ours was that rush of feeling that comes when a cat—or any other living creature—separates itself from the general throng of "cats" or "dogs" or "children" and becomes *your* cat, *your* dog, *your* child. I found myself gazing out the back doors anxiously, sometimes, if it seemed longer than it should have been since Bruiser had last shown up. I'd never had an outdoor cat before, and I worried about him getting into fights with rats or other cats or maybe even raccoons—or one of any number of worse things that might happen to him out there, alone and unprotected.

Bruiser was clearly a cat on a quest, and his holy grail was the thawing of Fanny's previously impervious heart. She may have played it cool at first, but she was now spending a larger portion of her days downstairs in the kitchen, rolling about in the sunlight that streamed through the back doors and persistently "come-hithering"—which is what Laurence and I call it when Fanny rolls halfway onto her back, all four paws in the air and, rather adorably, rubs the back of her head against whatever surface she happens to be lying on, looking at us with coquettish eyes that say, *Pet me! Love me!* (Occasionally Fanny will "come-hither" atop the third-floor balustrade, which overlooks a yawning three-story drop, and my heart climbs into my throat.)

Technically, she may have been doing this for Laurence and me. But the come-hithering always seemed to have started before I entered the room, and—although she never looked at him directly while she was doing it—Bruiser was always there with his face to the glass, watching Fanny with rapt attention. I knew beyond any doubt that Fanny was officially #TeamBruiser the afternoon when, upon spying him waiting for her outside the French doors and clutching an emptied toilet-paper roll in his mouth, she gave him the "bend-and-oof!," which is Fanny's highest mark of esteem—one that had previously been reserved almost exclusively for me, and occasionally for Laurence.

The "bend" part of the bend-and-oof! consists of Fanny stretching her front paws all the way out in front of her, pressing her chin and chest to the ground and raising her little rump high in the air, her long black tail held parallel to her body so that its tip grazes the middle of the top of her head. It looks very much like a deep bow—as if Fanny were a courtier paying homage to a sovereign in a royal court. The "oof!" part comes in when Fanny, without fully rising back into a standing position, stretches her front and hind legs even farther and flops hard onto her left side (which always provokes from Laurence and me an involuntary "*Oof!*").

And when Fanny did the bend-and-oof! for Bruiser—something she'd never done even for Clayton, it should be noted—it felt definitive. Fanny was smitten. She began peering through the back doors as anxiously as I did, if it felt that it had been too long since Bruiser's last appearance. When he'd finally reappear, either the come-hither or the bend-and-oof! was promptly deployed before the charmed eyes of a captivated Bruiser, the eagerness of his gaze mirrored in Fanny's own. Fanny even began leaving the occasional gift of her own on our side of the door, standing before the glass and waiting patiently with Rosie the Rat, her favorite toy, hanging from her mouth until Bruiser showed up with some present of his own, each of them dropping their respective booty and nudging it toward the glass at the same time, as if they really and truly were trying to exchange gifts.

"This is *fascinating*," I'd say to Laurence, if he happened to be in the kitchen with me while a gift exchange unfolded. "Don't you find this completely fascinating?" Laurence, however, rarely had much of a reply beyond a noncommittal grunt.

Laurence didn't want a third cat, and Clayton didn't either (at least, not this particular third cat). Fanny may have gazed adoringly at Bruiser—her big, strong, wild-at-heart "bad boy"—but Clayton was entirely unforgiving on the subject of Bruiser's abuse of our trees and plants. Sometimes he'd switch from his angry squeaking at Bruiser—which Bruiser persisted in ignoring—to squeak with equal anger at Fanny. *Stop encouraging him! It's just gonna make him pee on our stuff even more!*

But Fanny was undeterred, and whatever was happening between her and Bruiser seemed—to me, at any rate—too big to be denied. And so, after three days of feeding Bruiser consistently—once in the morning, and once in the afternoon—I went to dig out the trap I'd invested in back when the mama feral and her kittens had made our backyard their home.

THE TRAPPING OF A feral cat is fairly simple in theory—provided the cat in question has never been snagged by a trap before (a cat will rarely allow himself to be trapped twice)—although it does require a certain amount of patience.

Our trap was a long, rectangular metal cage with a front "door" that could be weighted down and fastened with a spring mechanism. The idea is to start out by placing food for the cat directly in front of the cage. As the days go by and you earn the cat's trust, you move the food just a little farther back with each feeding—until, eventually, the food is set far enough into the cage that the cat, in attempting to reach it, will trip the spring mechanism and cause the cage door to snap shut behind him. The key is to feed the cat at the same times every day, which hypothetically ensures that you trap the cat you mean to and not an opportunistic interloper who happens by and spots the food—or something else that isn't a cat at all. Most experienced TNR rescuers have stories about finding possums and raccoons in their traps, and I didn't relish the prospect of waking up one morning to a ticked-off raccoon I'd snared unwittingly.

But I'll admit that I was, by this time, thoroughly caught up in the romance of this wild cat who might allow himself to be tamed for love of Fanny. If the price of fostering true love was the possibility that I'd have to stare down an incensed varmint or two, then that was a risk I was willing to take.

Which isn't to say that I was at all sure Bruiser even could be tamed or socialized. I knew the challenges—possibly insurmountable—in trying to get an outdoor cat used to indoor life. But, at a minimum, it would be irresponsible to allow things to continue on as they were. So I calculated in my head the number of feedings it would take to get Bruiser all the way into the back of the cage, where he could be trapped, and scheduled a tentative appointment with our vet to have Bruiser neutered on the day I thought we were likely to catch him.

I also planned to create a backyard shelter for Bruiser, which I thought I'd line with soft towels and blankets. It would be good—imperative, even—for him to have a safe space of his own, where he could be protected from other critters and the worst of the weather while we gained his trust. And I had an idea that if I gradually started introducing household items and things with our scent on them—like old T-shirts—into that shelter, it might over time ease Bruiser's misgivings about us and possibly help us coax him indoors.

There are all kinds of ways to go about creating a snug, warm shelter for an outdoor cat, and after considering various possibilities I found on the Internet, I ultimately decided to get a large Styrofoam cooler, securely tape down the lid, and cut an entry hole into one side. It would be warm and waterproof, and while I wasn't sure how it would fare once heavier snows set in come winter, I was optimistic that, by then, Bruiser would have joined us indoors.

Bruiser didn't seem to be showing any wariness where the trap was concerned, which came as a relief. Each time I moved his food a scooch farther back in, he'd gamely enter the trap to get to it. The afternoon before the morning when I thought we'd finally be able to set the food all the way in the back and trap Bruiser once and for all, I went to our local hardware store to pick up a cooler, planning to spend the afternoon building Bruiser's new—albeit hopefully temporary—home.

I was just rounding the corner of my block on my return trip from the hardware store, cooler in hand, when I saw the flyer stapled to a telephone pole. It featured a black-and-white photo of a cat that was unmistakably Bruiser—floppy ear and all. Beneath the photo was an inscription that implored: SKIPPY IS MISSING. PLEASE HELP ME FIND HIM!

Bruiser, our mysterious backyard bad boy—the cool, hard-luck drifter who'd charmed Fanny and me despite the objections from the men in our lives—was, in fact, Skippy the housecat. And right behind this swift realization came another.

Fanny was going to be heartbroken.

According to the sign, Bruiser—aka "Skippy"—hailed from the Paulus Hook neighborhood, which was a good thirty-minute walk from our own part of Jersey City. Skippy (I realized I'd have to stop calling him "Bruiser") had covered quite a bit of ground for a cat—and for reasons I'd undoubtedly never know—to find our rose bushes and our Fanny. When I walked into the house, Fanny was waiting doggedly at her post before the French doors for the mystery cat's reappearance, Rosie the Rat held patiently in her mouth in anticipation of the afternoon's exchange of presents.

Poor thing! I thought as I reached for the phone—and wondered if feline girls, like human girls, were partial to ice cream and the Nora Ephron oeuvre when their romances came to abrupt ends. I thought that I might need some consolation myself. The prospect of adding another cat to our family had been growing on me, and I was surprised at the sharpness of the jab I'd felt in my chest when I'd realized that Bruiser wasn't going to be ours, that he'd never really been ours in the first place.

I dialed the number I'd seen on the poster, and the woman who answered sounded significantly older than I was. "Skippy's been spending a lot of time in our backyard," I told her, the name feeling odd and uncomfortable in my mouth. "If you come by tomorrow, I should be able to return him to you."

THE WINDOW OF MY little writing nook on the second floor of our house overlooks the backyard, so when the trap finally sprang the next morning—with Skippy safely inside—I heard it as soon as it happened. Although, even if I hadn't heard the trap's front entrance snap close, the loud, piteous wail the tuxedo cat sent up would have been a more than adequate tip-off. I raced downstairs to the kitchen and over to the French doors, where Fanny was pacing anxiously back and forth, her eyes fixed on Skippy in his cage. *Help him!* the look in her eyes beseeched as she turned them toward me. *He's in trouble!*

Opening the doors and shooing Fanny away from them (I didn't want her to get any ideas about darting into the backyard), I lugged the trap containing Skippy—who must have weighed a good fifteen pounds at least—into the kitchen. One of the more effective ways of calming a trapped cat is to throw a clean towel or blanket over the trap, and I had just such a towel at the ready, waiting on the kitchen counter.

But I didn't sling it over the cage—not right away. I couldn't help it. The romance between Fanny and Bruiser/Skippy had been building for nearly ten days up to this precise moment—the moment when the two of them would, at long last, meet face to face and nose to nose, with no glass separating them. They'd be able to touch paws for real, if they wanted to. That this meeting would take place through the metal bars of a cat trap—Fanny on one side of the bars, her backyard boyfriend on the other—added a poignancy to the moment that hadn't been there when, days ago, I'd imagined this first meeting and Fanny's joy at being united with her true love at last.

Skippy kept up his miserable wail from within the cage, striving unsuccessfully to huddle himself into a corner. I found myself remembering my own "bad boy" from years and years ago. He'd called me from jail very late one night, having been arrested for some minor infraction or other, and as twenty-one-year-old me had raced down to the police department to bail him out—through the darkness and deserted streets that had made it seem as if there were nothing in the entire world other than me, my car, and the man I was on my way to rescue—there had seemed to be a kind of wild and irresistible romance to the whole affair.

When I'd arrived, however, his bail had been more than I could afford to cover, so I'd been forced to call his mother, an unexpectedly distinguished lady who showed up in a Chanel suit as crisp and immaculate at two in the morning as it would have been at two in the afternoon. When she'd finally posted bail and the cop on duty had brought my boyfriend out, there was a look on her face that would have withered flowers in springtime. Upon seeing his mother, my bad boy instantly burst into tears. And . . . somehow he suddenly didn't seem nearly so "edgy" or "cool" anymore. As I collected my purse and the raincoat I'd thrown on over my sleep-wear and crept out of the police station, unnoticed by either of them, I remember telling myself, *Well . . . I guess that's that.*

Perhaps some similar feeling was operating in Fanny now—or maybe, even for cats, it's sometimes true that the anticipation of a moment turns out to better than the moment itself, when it finally arrives. Skippy's cries of misery continued to echo throughout the kitchen as Fanny tentatively approached the cage and inhaled a few cautious sniffs of it and the cat it contained. And then, curling her lips and raising a front paw into the air, she hissed loudly and smacked furiously at the cage as Skippy, pausing for breath at last, flinched ever farther back into his little corner and regarded her with yellow eyes filled with sadness and reproach.

"Fanny!" I cried. I'd never seen Fanny hiss or swipe at anybody. "That's your friend! Don't you recognize him?"

But it would seem that Fanny did not—or maybe she did, but seeing her wild, rebellious tom reduced to a caged and crying creature didn't suit her ideas of what a proper boyfriend should be. In any case, she hissed again and slapped the cage once more for good measure, then wheeled around and tore up the kitchen stairs, colliding with Clayton, who'd been on his way down to see what all the ruckus was about.

"*Women,*" I said to Skippy in the now-silent kitchen. "Am I right?" And then, pausing a beat to await a rueful chuckle of agreement that obviously never came, I sighed and tossed the clean towel over the cage, which seemed to settle Skippy down considerably.

Skippy's human came by to collect him two hours later, a gray-haired woman who'd been in Jersey City for decades before the mass migration from Manhattan—and its outrageously high rents—that had swept in relative newcomers like Laurence and me. She easily transferred Skippy's bulk from the cage into the cat carrier she'd brought with her. At the sight of his mom, the cat had once again taken up his doleful cries, although the familiarity of his own carrier appeared to soothe him, and from its dark recesses I could see his golden eyes, calmer now, blinking out at me.

"You know," I said tentatively to the woman—not liking to insert an opinion I hadn't been asked for, but having feelings on the subject strong enough that I couldn't resist saying *something*—"he might stick closer to home" (*and not spray so much,* I thought but didn't say) "if maybe you had him neutered?" I heard my voice go up at the end of the sentence, as if my sentence were a question—as if it might sound less judgmental that way.

Which, of course, it didn't.

The woman smiled at me sadly. "My husband didn't believe in neutering animals," she said. "He passed away about a year ago."

"I'm so sorry," I said, and let the matter drop.

"He was crazy about Skippy," she added. "Thank you so much for bringing him back to me." And then, refusing the twenty she tried to press into my hand, I let her out and closed the door behind her. There was a wrenching feeling in my belly as I realized that I would never see the tuxedo cat's little face, with its floppy little ear, waiting for Fanny and me at our door ever again.

Well, I thought—as I had twenty-five years earlier, following another mother-son jailbreak—*I guess that's that.*

FANNY KEPT UP A vigil at the French doors for the next few days, peering out—with an eager enthusiasm that began to dull as one day passed into the next—for signs of a familiar tuxedo tom who was no longer there, bearing gifts that no longer came. I wondered if Fanny realized that Skippy, the caged cat she'd hissed and swiped at, had in fact been the Bruiser she'd admired so. I wondered if maybe she now regretted how she'd acted, if she might be hoping for a second chance to do things differently. I thought that perhaps Fanny was learning something that humans also end up learning the hard way: that second chances are made all the sweeter by how very rare they tend to be.

At the end of a week, a new cat turned up in our yard. He had long, magnificent smoky-gray fur and bottle-green eyes. When he squatted to pee next to our tree, this time it was Fanny and not Clayton who reacted with anger, who reared up on her hind legs to hiss and snarl and strike angrily at the glass with one velvety black paw. *Go away! That's where* Bruiser *likes to pee!*

"Oh, Fanny," I said, kneeling down to scritch affectionately behind her ears. "It'll get easier. 'Tis better to have loved and lost . . ."

Without even looking at me, Fanny struck at the glass once more, then turned to stalk upstairs in a huff.

"Yeah," I said to her retreating backside. "I never really bought that one either."

Toy Stories

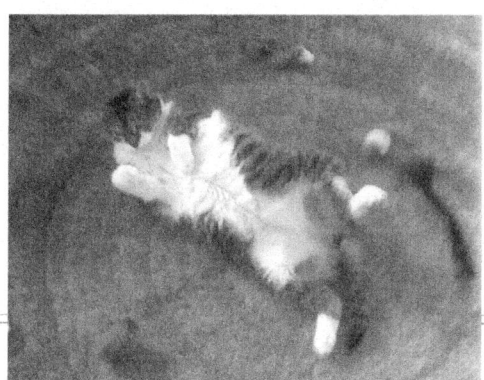

CAT AND MOUSE

For a long time, I believe that cats didn't really like traditional cat toys.

I thought that the only reason such toys existed at all was so that cat parents could make themselves happy by purchasing something they thought might make their cats happy—a cat's unbounded enthusiasm (*Hey! You actually did something right!*) being the Holy Grail of adoring cat slaves everywhere. And when the cats, inevitably, reacted with predictable indifference to the toy itself, and proceeded to amuse themselves with the bag the toy came in, their indulgent human's shoulders might sag a bit with disappointment, but ultimately they'd be cheered by the certain knowledge that they certainly weren't any *more* inept than scores of other bumbling owners of hard-to-please cats the world over.

I believed this because the one thing all three of my "first generation" cats—widely varying from each other in all other matters of personality, temperament, and taste—could agree on was that cat toys, as a general rule, were stupid. There would be the occasional hit—Homer's beloved toy worm being the most conspicuous example—but the hits were far outnumbered by the misses. Scores of toy mice and plastic balls and flying feathered things attached to strings and sticks, and all manner of other doodads and geegaws, found their way over the years from shopping bag to floor to trash can in pristine, unused condition, while the receipts for the toys' purchase (*Hooray! A crumpled ball of paper!*) were usually good for at least an afternoon's worth of entertainment.

It was a full seventeen years into my life as a "cat mom" before I realized how very wrong I was to apply the preferences of my first three cats to all cats generally—because one of the first things I learned about Clayton and Fanny as kittens was that they simply adored cat toys. *Loved* them. Couldn't get enough. They went nuts for cat toys with all the passionate ardor of a human child opening presents on Christmas morning. Clayton was partial to crinkle balls and little plastic springs that bounced zanily when thrown around the room, whereas Fanny preferred toys that resembled actual living creatures—such as toy mice, or anything with feathers.

But, ultimately, just about anything was enough to make them happy, so long as it was a toy that had been meant for cats. I'd come home from the pet store with a bag of goodies that I'd intended to trickle out over the course of days or weeks, but Clayton and Fanny would follow me around so persistently—as if I were an inexplicably tightfisted Santa Claus—and wail so piteously until the shopping bag had been entirely emptied of its contents, that it was impossible to refuse them. Dozens of toys would thus end up scattered around the living room in one glorious burst of largesse—so that our home resembled a feline version of *Babes in Toyland*—to be played with for, perhaps, a full minute or two, before my tiny tormentors would grow bored with their bounty and look at me expectantly as if to say, *Aren't there any more?* Eventually, Laurence would enter the living room—his bare foot connecting painfully with the business end of a plastic spring or some such thing—and he'd calmly observe, "*WHY DO YOU KEEP BUYING THEM SO MANY $@#*$# TOYS?!!?*" at which point I'd throw a token handful into a bag to be stored in a closet, until the whole cycle repeated itself again a week or two later.

(Lest you judge me, gentle reader, let me ask you this: If you had two cats who it was actually *easy* to make happy—who would leap and cavort with unbounded joy for a mere ten or fifteen dollars' worth of felt and plastic—would you be able to hold out longer than a couple of weeks before indulging both them and yourself again?)

Sometimes I'd get the bright idea of trying to sneak the toys in unnoticed, so that I could distribute them on my own schedule and thus prolong the cats' pleasure, as well as my own. Fanny had a deep instinct for sensing shenanigans, however, and would insist on always greeting me at the door—poking her nose deeply into every box or bag I came home with—which made concealment, as a practical matter, impossible.

The kittens had just turned a year old—thus officially graduating from "kittens" to "cats"—when I published a novel written from a rescue cat's point of view, and elected to go on a national reading tour of no-kill shelters rather than the standard author tour of bookstores. I found corporate sponsors who agreed to donate food and litter to all of the shelters I visited, and many of my readers got in on the action, too—mailing me hand-crocheted "catghans," little sachets of catnip, and the like, to distribute among the cats at the shelters along my route.

And one generous reader sent an enormous box full of cat toys. I wasn't sure what was in the box at first—it was so large and so heavy that I assumed it was a shipment of books from my publisher—which was why I made the fatal error of opening it while Clayton and Fanny were present, revealing a veritable Aladdin's cave to the dazzled eyes of my two concupiscent kitties. Nestled among the bonanza of feline playthings was a plastic bag containing, easily, a hundred or so of the little felt-covered toy mice that were Fanny's absolute favorite plaything in the whole world.

Fanny, being a cat, certainly couldn't count. But she could plainly see at a glance that this box held more little toy mice than she'd ever seen at one time, or even imagined that she ever would see at one time, in her entire life. She began cavorting wildly—rearing up on her hind legs and dancing around in circles—the sum total of all her dreams and desires distilled down to a single, fervent wish: *Give me all those toy mice RIGHT NOW! RIGHT NOW RIGHT NOW RIGHT NOW!*

For once, though, I held firm. "These toys aren't for you," I told Fanny. "They're for the poor kitties in shelters who don't have a mom to buy toys for them." It's not that I thought Fanny would actually understand what I was saying—or that she would find my logic persuasive even if she could. But I did hope that the unusually steady tone of my voice (because at least half the time when I said "no" to my cats, there was still the hint of an eventual "yes" to come) would convey that her getting into this particular toy box was going to be a non-starter.

And it appeared, at first, that I'd been somewhat successful at carrying the point. Fanny almost immediately stopped her dancing and capering, siting on her haunches to eye me with disappointment for a moment before following me into Laurence's home office—where I carefully placed the box of toys on the very highest shelf of the very tallest bookcase we had. I was wary of putting the box into a closet, as all of our closets had sliding doors, which Fanny knew perfectly well how to manipulate open. Surely, I thought, even Fanny—by far the most daring gymnast of a cat I'd ever lived with—wouldn't be able to scale her way to the top of a six-foot bookcase.

It wasn't the first time I'd ever been impressed by a determined cat's ingenuity, and it certainly wouldn't be the last. I'm still not sure how she managed to accomplish it—and I'll admit to having been filled with a certain wondering admiration as I tried to imagine what the process might have been, even as I surveyed the end results with dismay. But, however it was that she'd pulled it off, the fact remains that Laurence and I came home from lunch at our favorite neighborhood sandwich place one day to find the box lying on the floor, its contents entirely spilled out. The plastic bag containing all the toy mice had been ripped open—and while the majority of them still remained (even Fanny couldn't quite pull off a hundred-mouse heist all by herself), at least twenty or thirty of them were nowhere to be seen.

Nowhere to be seen *at that precise moment*, I should say, because as the days and weeks went by, they began to resurface. Fanny may have been a bit of a sneak thief (*may have been*, or *definitely was?*) who'd concealed her purloined goods so cleverly that I never did find her hiding place. But she also had something of the generous spirit of a Robin Hood in her—albeit a reverse Robin Hood of sorts, one who, instead of stealing money from the rich to give to the needy, rather stole toys from the needy and redistributed them to the middle-class. Not even to the middle class *generally*, but to one *specific* middle-class family that, truth be told, already had more toys than they knew what to do with, and was somewhat mortified to think that they were getting all these new toys at the expense of the kitten equivalent of an orphanage.

Maybe Robin Hood isn't the best comparison. The point is that while Fanny was indisputably a thief and a hoarder, she also unquestionably was—and remains— a generous little soul. What we learned about Fanny—whose personality, at only a year old, we were still discovering—in the wake of her first successful caper was that she delighted in bestowing gifts with a free hand upon those she loved.

When Laurence and I first began finding little gray toy mice in unexpected places, we thought that Fanny had simply dropped them carelessly wherever she'd happened to tire of playing with them. But it soon became clear that the places in which we found them were too deliberate—and the timing of when we'd discover them was too consistent—to be the result of accident or chance. There would be matching mice on our pillows when we went to bed at night, and a mouse thoughtfully placed on the bathmat directly in front of the shower or bathroom sink when we got up in the morning. If I set the table ahead of dinner and then turned my back for a few minutes to attend to food preparations, I'd turn around again to see that Laurence and I each had a little toy mouse awaiting us on our dinner plates. (Perhaps Fanny thought we might enjoy a pre-dinner *amuse-bouche*?) Laurence and I would sit down to work early in the day to find that matching toy mice had been placed square in the middle of our computer keyboards, and I began to take it for granted that—when my work for the day was done, and I was ready to pick up a good book for an hour or two—a mouse would be waiting for me atop whatever novel I happened to be reading at the moment. I learned to check thoroughly the pair of shoes that I wore most often—the ones that I kept near the front door for easy access—for any faux-rodent stowaways before putting them on, after being uncomfortably surprised a couple of times when sliding my feet into them unawares.

"Thank you, Fanny," I always made a point of saying whenever I found her latest offering—because inevitably Fanny would be waiting nearby to see how her "gift" was received.

"You're just reinforcing a bad habit," Laurence admonished me once.

"Technically, sharing is a *good* habit," I replied. "It's the stealing that was bad."

Clayton and Homer (who was still with us then) weren't left out of this Mouse-A-Palooza. They, too, would arrive at favored sleeping spots to be greeted by the grey felt and little pink ears of a tiny toy mouse. Homer was completely uninterested in these particular playthings; they didn't have bells that made engaging sounds, and they didn't smell like anything distinctive, and the fact that they *looked* like mice meant, of course, less than nothing to him. But Clayton—while not being nearly as partial to toy mice (at least, the kind that didn't make a rattling sound) as he was to crinkle balls and plastic springs—could usually be counted on to bat around Fanny's gift mouse for a minute or two before nosing it aside and sprawling out for a catnap.

I couldn't help but be touched at the way Fanny remembered her brothers when it came to gift-giving. Laurence said I was nuts, but I thought it showed real character and altruism on her part. "If anything ever happens to us," I'd tell him, "Fanny's the one who'll take care of the others."

"Good luck with that," was Laurence's invariable response.

Soon enough, there were so many little gray mice littering our home that, even by *my* standards, it was a bit absurd. I picked them up and squirreled them away, secreting them in hidden drawers, when Fanny wasn't looking. It seemed like a waste to throw them in the trash—but of course, now that they could only be classified as "gently used" rather than "brand new," I couldn't apply them to their original purpose, i.e. distributing them to the shelter cats I'd be visiting along my tour stops.

I'd known the instant I saw what Fanny had done that I'd have to replace them. I was less concerned about the expense (although even an inexpensive toy, when purchased in large numbers, becomes a real investment) than I was in getting them into the house and then out to the shelters without being...intercepted...by my wily little feline trickster. For the first time, I regretted being the kind of goody-goody kid who'd never grown experienced in the art of sneaking contraband into her parents' house.

What I finally ended up doing was purchasing the toy mice from my local pet store (cleaning out their entire stock, to the effusive delight of the owner), triple-wrapping them in plastic bags, concealing *that* in the largest purse I owned, and ferreting the entire stash into my own home office, swiftly bypassing Fanny upon my arrival back at our apartment—although the one bag that routinely came into the house without being inspected by Fanny was my purse. (*There's never anything in there but boring human stuff,* was likely Fanny's philosophy on the matter.) Behind my closed office door, I then immediately packaged the smuggled mice into a series of boxes I'd pre-addressed to shelters. My original plan had been to distribute in person the goodies that readers had sent me for the cats on my tours tops—but, no matter how cleverly I might hide them, clearly the toy mice weren't safe for any length of time in a house inhabited by my felonious Fanny.

The plan went off without a hitch, and a few weeks later my tour commenced. At every tour stop, the staff and volunteers who ran the shelters I visited would thank me for the toy mice I'd mailed them a month or so back. I was always quick to supply the name of the reader who they were really from, without going into details about why those toys, specifically, had preceded my visit by several weeks, when everything else my sponsors and readers donated had arrived at the same time I did.

Like the mom of any budding young criminal, I was anxious to shield Fanny's wrongdoing from public scrutiny.

So I'd keep the conversations light and innocuous. "I hope your cats enjoy the toy mice," I'd say. "My cat is absolutely *crazy* for them."

A Fairy Tale

Back in the late Nineties and the Aughts—before video streaming had taken hold, when DVD was the premiere format for home-video viewing—film studios would spend lavishly on a DVD launch. There were out-of-town press junkets—which Laurence, as the DVD/Video editor for *Variety* magazine, was flown out to attend, all expenses paid, as a matter of course—extravagant launch parties, and an endless array of creative tchotchkes and swag that diligent publicists mailed out to reviewers along with the review copy of the DVD itself. Laurence still has much of this curio lining his shelves, and—along with an assortment of film-branded keychains, notepads, money clips, snow globes, baseball caps, jackets, and t-shirts—he's also the proud owner of a stuffed Sharktopus, three rubber ears (one from *Blue Velvet*, one from *Vincent & Theo*, and one from a Vincent Van Gogh documentary), a box of Bernie Mac 'n' Cheese, a copy of *The Joy of Cooking* "autographed" by Hannibal Lechter, *Sid and Nancy* pens designed to look like hypodermic needles, a stress ball shaped like a woman's breast from some Russ Meyer movie or other, *Being John Malkovich*-branded Russian nesting dolls, a can of *Species* green slime, and on and on and on.

He also once had a Lucite picture frame that had been sent out with the *Swimfan* DVD (a sort of *Fatal Attraction* for the high-school set). It contained a hidden button that, when pressed, would trigger a recording and cause the frame to shriek: "*YOU LOVE ME, I KNOW IT!!!*" Laurence filled the frame with a collage of funny pictures of himself and gave it to me as a gag gift to place on my desk, back when I was still working in an office; co-workers stopping by my cubicle and innocently asking, "Oh, is this your boyfriend?" as they picked up the frame were usually in for a startling moment.

It was 2008, or thereabouts, when Disney decided to launch a "Fairies" franchise with a collection of straight-to-video cartoon movies, which I think they were hoping to make as big a *thing* among as the Disney "Princess" franchise. Tinkerbell was the familiar face fronting this new endeavor, and she was given a collection of ethnically diverse fairy friends with names like Iridessa and Silvermist. Disney spared no expense for the launch party, held in an event space overlooking Bryant Park that had been transformed into a fairyland with pink and green lighting, glitter galore, shimmering ice sculptures, a generous assortment of high-priced delicacies for attendees to munch on, and—perhaps most crucially to the success of any New York media event—an unlimited open bar.

So Laurence was a bit disappointed when he saw the swag Disney offered attendees to go home with at the end of the evening—a collection of colorful laminated bookmarks with pictures and whimsical descriptions of the newly minted fairies that said things like, "Rosetta, a garden-talent fairy, was one of the first arrivals in

Pixie Hollow and shares a sassy streak with her friend Tinkerbell." The bookmarks featured iridescent glitter (or "fairy dust") that had been pressed between the lamination and the cardboard of the bookmark itself.

"Oh...they're giving out bookmarks," Laurence said, with the glumness of a kid who's gotten socks for Christmas, as he looked through his gift bag—while I, at the same moment and with unfeigned enthusiasm, exclaimed, "Cool! *Bookmarks!*"

I was obviously aged well beyond the target demo for the Disney "Fairies" franchise; still, a compulsive reader like me can never have too many bookmarks—especially sturdy ones.

My new bookmarks were sturdy, indeed, and seemed likely to withstand for years to come even the overuse to which I will typically put a bookmark. They also made a pleasing sort of reverberating *whoosh*-y sound—bending partially and then quickly whipping back out straight—when held in one hand and waved back and forth rapidly, which I discovered one day while doing just that with idle inattention while reading a book on the sofa. I was pulled from my reading reverie not by the sound that the bookmark made as I waved it around, but rather by a particularly insistent squeak coming from the coffee table right next to me.

Mildly surprised—it was unusual for her to disturb me while I was reading—I looked over and saw Vashti sitting close to me on the coffee table. Her eyes were enormous and all pupil, and she was staring with fixed, murderous attention at the bookmark waving in my hand, her head moving quickly from right to left in perfect time with the bookmark's movements.

I couldn't help but laugh. "Whatsamatter, Vashti?" I said. "You want *this*? You want *this*?" I waved the bookmark back and forth at a faster pace, and Vashti promptly reared up onto her hind legs while slashing her front paws at the bookmark furiously, even attempting to catch it with her teeth whenever she thought she had a clear shot at it.

It should be noted that Vashti was never a particularly blood-lusty cat. In fact, now that I think about it, that afternoon might have been the first time I'd seen Vashti's pupils dilate other than as a reaction to the amount of sun in the room. Back when we lived with Jorge in Miami, and Vashti used to catch geckos on our sunporch, she always promptly released them unharmed—seemingly more interested in the sport of snagging them than in anything more predatory. In all the years I'd lived with her, she'd never once unsheathed her claws, even in play, except occasionally to grab onto the fabric of a sofa or chair she might be in danger of tumbling off of. And while she'd enjoyed playing fetch with a crumpled-up ball of paper when she was little, she'd never shown any interest in more traditional cat toys, like felt-covered mice or little balls with feathered tails—which I'd always assumed was because she had limited-to-zero interest in killing any mice or feathered creatures in real life. She'd never "chittered" at birds who landed on our windowsills, or pounced on my fingers when I'd wiggled them enticingly under a bedsheet, or sprung out at me from under a bed in a surprise attack—not even when she was a kitten.

It seems almost impossible to imagine a cat with absolutely no instinctive prey drive whatsoever. But Vashti had always appeared to me to be exactly that—a cat who simply didn't have it in her even to wound, much less kill, anything.

So it was entirely novel, and more than a little amusing, to see Vashti—at long last, and at the ripe old age of twelve—provoked into a homicidal rage by a glittery, intensely girly, laminated Disney Fairies bookmark.

Laurence and I were tickled by Vashti's sudden, if limited, new violent streak. To see our sweet, mild-mannered girl, who'd never-ever even attempted to hurt a fly before (literally—flies would buzz around Vashti's head, and she'd observe them with placid, sweet-tempered restraint), finally unsheathe her claws and pull back snarling lips to reveal her sharp little teeth—to demonstrate that she did in fact have some of the same lethal impulses as any other cat—became a reliable form of entertainment for all of us. I promptly transferred my stash of bookmarks from the Disney gift bag in my closet to the coffee table, so they'd be at the ready whenever Vashti leapt from floor to table and looked pointedly from the bookmarks to me and then back again. *Wave it around,* her eyes eloquently demanded, *so I can kill it!* And Laurence—who Vashti had firmly wrapped around her little white paw, and who'd never been able to deny her anything that might give her pleasure—would sit through entire two-hour movies on the couch without ever once pausing as he waved a Fairies bookmark from side to side before a tantalized, and seemingly enraged, Vashti's face.

What I think we got a kick out of—even more than watching Vashti attack those bookmarks with so much fierce determination—was the way she would reliably rear up on her hind legs, as soon as the bookmarks went airborne, into what I called her "Abominable Snow Kitty" pose. Her front paws would swipe furiously in a *whap!-whap!-whap!-whap!-whap!*, as if she were one of the Three Stooges administering punishment to a fellow Stooge, while her back paws, struggling to support her full weight all by themselves, moved in a complicated sort of boxer's dance. "Oh no, it's *the Abominable Snow Kitty!*" I'd cry—and sometimes, unable to resist the temptation, I'd even sink my fingers into the exposed, thick white fluff of her belly, so rarely seen (particularly as Vashti wasn't one to sleep on her back with her belly exposed). And Vashti, usually so quick to preen and purr when given any sort of admiring attention, would merely pause briefly in her pursuit of a Fairies bookmark to give me a quick look of irritation. *Leave me alone—I'm trying to kill something!*

I'd thought that these extra-durable bookmarks would take me through years of reading—that the only reason I might eventually have to replace them with newer, flimsier alternatives would be as I inevitably lost them to the general havoc of books and papers that tend to accumulate on any and all surfaces of a home shared by two writers.

But, alas, it was not to be. Tough as the Fairy bookmarks were, they were no match for the persistent abuse to which Vashti subjected them. The lamination began to fray and peel back at the edges, revealing the original cardboard of the bookmark itself. Puncture wounds from Vashti's teeth pierced right through the lamination in some places, leaving gaping holes. Often we'd come home to find that Vashti, having grown impatient in waiting for us to return and wave around one of the bookmarks for her, had taken matters into her own paws and pilfered the coffee-table stash on her own—leaving a wreckage of bent and bruised Fairy bookmarks scattered about the living-room rug like the casualties from a particularly brutal bookmark war.

Things took a particularly grim turn the night we got home to find that one bookmark bore a perfectly round hole—clearly inflicted by a feline canine tooth—smack in the middle of the forehead of a fairy named Fawn. (*Gentle as a fawn, she was!*) The smiling, fragile, wide-eyed face of a delicate little fairy who appeared to have been shot, execution-style, at point-blank range through the head was a sobering sight, indeed.

"This is why we can't have nice things," Laurence observed dryly, to which I retorted, "The cats *are* our 'nice things.'"

By this point, the bookmarks weren't much good for marking books anymore. They were too bent and warped to lie flat, and lying flat is pretty much a bookmark's entire *raison d'etre*. Most of them were too limp and twisted even to make the reverberating *whoosh*-y sound that had attracted Vashti's notice in the first place. Nevertheless, we still kept a couple on our coffee table, because from time to time Vashti would remember how much she'd always wanted to murder those wretched fairies, and now that they were useless anyway there didn't seem to be any reason to keep her from descending on them at will.

One afternoon, Laurence's cousin came over with her young daughter, Allison. Allison was almost like a fairy-child herself, with long, Alice-in-Wonderland blond hair and enormous, liquidy brown eyes. Those eyes filled with tears as they caught sight of the remains of the Fairy bookmarks—the fairies still smiling with persistent sweetness from behind the cracked and cloudy remnants of the lamination that had once protected them. The bookmarks still shimmered with the glittery "fairy dust" that had been pressed between lamination and cardboard when they were first made, although there was a mournful quality to the glittery sparkle now, given how bedraggled the rest of the package was. "They were so pretty!" Allison blurted out, a single tear falling from her eye.

I thought that Allison was mourning the Fairy bookmarks themselves. (What little girl could be expected to maintain her composure upon catching sight of a slew of murdered fairies?) But the next time she came over, she had a gift for me—a brand-new bookmark. Obviously made for very young girls, this bookmark featured a plastic-pouch coating that contained a viscous sort of liquid, in which was suspended more glitter than I would have thought a single bookmark could hold. "She felt so bad for you when she saw what the cat did to your other bookmarks," her mom told Laurence and me. "She bought this for you from her allowance."

I was touched. "It's *beautiful*," I told Allison, stooping to plant a kiss on her cheek. "I love it. Thank you so much."

We were all going out to do something or other in the city that day—likely something related to my wedding, which was now only a couple of months away—and, without thinking about it, I carelessly left Allison's bookmark on the coffee table unattended as we all sailed happily out the door.

It was a mistake. I realized the full gravity of my error a couple of hours later, when I returned home to find the dried husk of the new bookmark lying in the middle of the living room rug, its plastic sac clawed open and entirely drained of liquid. Not too far away from it was a miserable Vashti, her snout and entire right flank drenched in iridescent glitter.

"Oh no!" I exclaimed. Frantically, I scooped Vashti up in one hand and bundled her toward the bathroom, pausing only to grab the phone in my other. I speed-dialed the vet as the tub ran, and put the phone on speaker as I attempted to navigate a now-struggling Vashti into the water.

It took a minute or so for the vet to be able to make sense of what, exactly, I was asking. My concern, naturally, was over whatever quantity of the glitter Vashti might have consumed in attempting to groom herself free of it. But the vet's feeling was that, since the bookmark was made for children, the glitter and the gel it had been suspended in were likely non-toxic.

She rattled off a few signs and symptoms I should be on the lookout for over the next few hours—vomiting, faintness, disorientation, and so on. None of them materialized, fortunately.

Still, Vashti's poop did sparkle in the litter box like fool's gold for nearly a week.

SLAP HAPPY

Life was hard for my poor Scarlett.

By this, I don't mean to imply that she suffered from any form of abuse of neglect, or that she was plagued by some chronic physical ailment that inflicted pain and suffering. Scarlett was a healthy girl for all but the last year of her life and, like all of my cats, she was wrapped up in a warm cocoon of pure love from the moment she came to me as a tiny kitten. If you've read this far into my cat chronicles, you probably know already that there isn't a whole lot I wouldn't do or haven't done—often well beyond the boundaries of what might fairly be called "sane"—to ensure that my cats are as contented and comfortable as conscientious care can make them.

What made life hard for Scarlett (and this was really no fault of her own, because she couldn't help being the way she was) was that absolutely everything was so *annoying*—so utterly *irritating*, so profoundly *vexing*—that just getting through her typical day could be a feline Bataan Death March of sorts in terms of the sheer agony inflicted upon her.

People were annoying—loud and oafish and apt to invite more of their kind over to disturb the sanctity her home—and eventually Scarlett would have to live with two of them. Other cats were also annoying, and Scarlett had to endure living with two of *them*, as well. She shared a litter box with those two cats, and not having an immaculately pristine litter box to step into each and every time nature called was annoying. So were the pigeons who landed along the windowsills of the apartments we lived in. Maybe to other cats, having birds to watch through a window counted as some form of entertainment—but not for Scarlett. Whenever the cooing head and pinkish eye of a feathered interloper dared to present itself at a window Scarlett happened to be near, she would sniff disdainfully at the lively interest shown by the other two cats (bona fide idiots, the both of them, as far as Scarlett was concerned) and stalk away with pointed hauteur.

The weather—which tended toward the too-hot and the too-cold far more often than it hit the sweet spot of "just right"—was annoying. Food was annoying, unless it was the exact kind of dry food Scarlett preferred—and when she ate too much of it, to the point that it caused health problems and was thus replaced exclusively with a moist option that the other two cats didn't seem to mind at all, that was supremely annoying. Cat condos were annoying because you had to climb them—*you had to* climb *them!*—and who had the time or interest for such an absurdity? Cat toys were annoying, and also stupid, unless maybe they were filled with catnip. But even then they were only tolerable until their catnip smell wore off, at which point—in their lumpish uselessness—they were *beyond* annoying.

In many ways, Scarlett reminded me of my mean-old-lady elementary school librarian, Mrs. Amdore—who had, for unfathomable reasons, spent nearly five decades as a children's librarian despite clear and daily evidence that she detested both children and children's books. (Although it should be noted that, at seventy years of age, Mrs. Amdore still rode a Harley to and from work every day—which all of us kids agreed was pretty badass.)

I will go to my grave insisting that Scarlett's nature contained hidden troves of sweetness that you had to know her intimately—and be willing to break through an awful lot of crustiness—to see. There were moments when, unexpectedly and unbidden, Scarlett would come to lie gently against my leg—resting her head on my knee and looking up into my face with a gaze that was equal parts love and world-weariness (*you know you're the only human for me, but why must life be soooooo excruciating?*)—and those were great, great moments, indeed.

But the indisputable fact remains that almost nobody ever saw any hint of that sweetness, except for me. (Ah, my poor, misunderstood girl!)

Scarlett eschewed almost every toy set before her for her amusement, and disliked the idea of playing with anyone else almost as much as she disliked the idea of playing at all. But there was one game—discovered when Scarlett was roughly ten months old, shortly before we adopted Vashti—that was both interactive and that Scarlett enjoyed immensely. It was actually pretty simple, as far as games went: I would crumple up a ball of paper and toss it to Scarlett. Scarlett would rise up on her hind legs like a prairie dog and, with her front left paw, slap the ball of paper back over to me, volleyball style. I would then pick up the ball of paper and throw it over to her again—and we'd lather/rinse/repeat until Scarlett decided it was Game Over, abruptly turning her back and striding coolly away with a single peremptory flick of her tail.

Naturally, when we adopted two kittens a year apart from each other, they each in their turn wanted to get in on whatever games the "big cat" was playing. Scarlett, it probably goes without saying, didn't play well with others. Vashti learned this lesson quickly and thoroughly, once Scarlett had doled out a half-dozen or so whaps on the head with an admonishing paw, after Vashti tried one too many times to insert herself into Scarlett's game.

Homer, on the other hand—ferociously bright as he was—couldn't seem to grasp this very simple point. The sound of a piece of paper crumpling into a ball drew him instantly to my side, and, at the sound of the paper going airborne, he'd follow its trajectory as fast as his four tiny paws could carry him, his sensitive ears following its path through the air—and inevitably leading him to plow directly into a hapless and thoroughly disgruntled Scarlett, who (poor thing!) had been minding her own business, not bothering anybody, and was only waiting for the paper ball to connect with her raised front paw so she could slap it back in my direction.

No matter how many times Scarlett snarled and hissed at Homer, or "disciplined" him with angry smacks of her paw about his ears and snout, Homer seemed entirely unable—or unwilling—to heed the lesson that this particular game was Scarlett's, and Scarlett's only. *This is MY special thing with Mom!* I imagined Scarlett thinking. *Why do you have to ruin everything?!!?*

Homer enriched my life immeasurably from the very first day I brought him home. But the same can hardly be said of Scarlett's experience with Homer. To Scarlett, he was simply The Ruiner of All Things—of the games she loved but that he interrupted, of the meals she could no longer enjoy with quiet dignity once Homer had nosily inserted himself into her dish for a quick inspection (*Hey! You have the same food I do! Cool!*), of the peaceful naps he inevitably interrupted, particularly as a playful kitten, with a beseeching invitation to join him in some game or other. The differences in their individual perceptions of their mutual relationship always fascinated me—because it was very clear that Homer genuinely believed Scarlett to be his very best friend. And it was equally clear that Scarlett regarded Homer as...well...*enemy* would certainly be putting it too strongly. But "best friends," from Scarlett's perspective, they most emphatically were not. That Scarlett might even want a best friend was undoubtedly as foreign a concept to her way of thinking as Chinese algebra.

The thought of Scarlett losing the one and only game that she actually found some pleasure in was distressing for me. I tried to find moments when Homer wasn't around or was otherwise occupied, so Scarlett and I could play a quick and quiet round of Slap the Paper Ball. But that was easier said than done. Homer was such a very "present" cat—almost always to be found at my side or somewhere in my immediate vicinity—that opportunities were few. I would try exhausting Homer with active play to the point that he finally collapsed in a heap on the couch, seemingly too worn out to so much as lift his head. But, no matter how exhausted he was, if Homer heard Scarlett playing, then he wanted to play, too. Sometimes, upon hearing Scarlett and me starting up a round of her favorite game, he'd be too tired to do much beyond creeping over to sit silently next to her—completely oblivious to the scathing looks of indignation and scorn that she turned his way—waiting for the paper ball I threw over to reach them. Scarlett would slap him with her paw, of course, and Homer would be undeterred by this—also of course—although he would obligingly move a few inches to his left or right, to give Scarlett a bit more breathing room, before turning his head toward me in anticipation. *Are you going to throw the paper ball or what?*

During the two-and-a-half years when my three cats and I were living in a one-room studio apartment, the game was given up entirely. There was no way, within such close quarters, to sneak in a round with Scarlett while Homer was out of earshot—simply because he never *was* out of earshot. But when we finally moved into Laurence's spacious three-bedroom apartment—positively palatial by the standards to which we had become accustomed—occasionally there would be moments. I'd leave Homer asleep on the couch, where he'd curled up next to me while I was reading a book, and tiptoe into the last bedroom at the far end of the apartment, where Scarlett was drowsing alone. I'd bring a pre-crumpled ball of paper (the sound of my crumpling the paper was always a telltale sign that a game would soon be afoot, and would wake Homer instantly), close the bedroom door behind me, and Scarlett's drowsiness would change to alert attention as she sensed that a rare moment when she could play—without Homer the Buttinsky inserting himself into the proceedings—had arrived.

Eventually, we would lose Scarlett to old age and the passage of years. It was more than pathetic—it was crushing—to see how the loss seemed to age Homer overnight into the little old man he technically was by then, but that he hadn't seemed to realize he was until Scarlett was gone. Even the sound of my wadding up a piece of paper couldn't rouse his interest. Nothing did, until we adopted two little kittens named Clayton and Fanny. Clayton was every bit as enamored of Homer as Homer had once been of Scarlett—and if there's such a thing as kitty karma, then the way that Clayton insisted on shadowing Homer's every waking moment and action was surely a what-goes-around-comes-around repayment for the way Homer had once obsessively tracked Scarlett's every move.

Homer was a friendlier cat than Scarlett had been, and the close attention actually seemed to benefit him more than otherwise. He unquestionably found Clayton irritating at first, and to see his own disciplinary front paw rise into the air before falling onto Clayton's nose in a resounding slap—a mirror image of the way Scarlett had once attempted to enforce courtesy with him—was amusing. But, soon enough, the kittens' playfulness coaxed Homer back into much of his own, and returned some much-needed joy into all of our hearts.

The one thing Homer was never able to abide, however, was when Clayton tried to take part in a game of Slap the Paper Ball.

He was more than willing to engage Clayton in a round of Chase Me, Then I'll Chase You, or a scrappy game of tug-of-war over a catnip toy, or to leap out at Clayton in the surprise ambushes that made Clayton positively squeal with delight before the two of them began to roll around the floor in a mock fight.

But Slap the Paper Ball became Homer's game, and Homer's only. Every time I threw a paper ball in Homer's direction, the three-legged Clayton would inevitably hippity-hop after it, bumping into Homer in cheerful anticipation of the new game they were about to play together. And Homer, in a lesson he'd learned well from Scarlett, would slap Clayton silly, as fiercely protective of the sanctity of this one—and only this one—game as Scarlett had ever been.

This was MY special thing with Scarlett and Mom, I imagined Homer admonishing Clayton. *Why do you have to ruin everything?!*

Daylight Cravings

THERE WERE A LOT of things to love about Homer, and it's probably safe to say that I've paid tribute in writing to just about all of them. It would be difficult, after all, to expend nearly a hundred and seventy-five thousand printed words on a cat without getting to most of his good qualities along the way. Homer's dazzling intelligence, his heroism and bravery, his high-spirited zest for life, the harmonic melody of his purr, the endearing *clip-clip* of his paws on the floors of our homes (Homer rarely allowing me to trim his claws) as he followed me from room to room, the way the back of his neck so often smelled like warm cinnamon cookies fresh from the oven (the mystery of how such a thing could even be possible confounding me to this day)—all this and far more have been duly noted and footnoted in the two books and some two-dozen short stories I've written about Homer to date.

But the one quality that I perhaps failed to do justice to in my writing—and that I definitely didn't appreciate as much as I should have at the time—is how accommodating Homer was. It's taken nearly a decade of my being in daily contact with thousands of other cat people, and close to seven years living with my two current imps, Clayton and Fanny, to come to realize just how rare and wondrous a quality accommodation is in a cat.

Cats, as everyone knows, are not generally considered easygoing, go-with-the-flow sorts of creatures. You can change your cat's schedule, his food, his feline (or human) roommate situation, his sleeping arrangements, the litter you put in his litter box, but you do so at your own peril—and possibly also at the peril of cherished possessions, which may end up as casualties in the war of attrition that's likely to ensue as your cat reasons, using infallible feline logic: *Maybe if I pee on/vomit on/claw up* this *sweater/sofa cushion/area rug, I'll get my way.*

But Homer somehow managed to be both the most feline of cats and also the very soul of accommodation—and if I failed to appreciate this quality in him sufficiently back then, I've come to cherish the memory of it now. Homer slept when I slept, uncomplainingly ate whatever and whenever I chose to feed him, bonded cheerfully with the other cats I made him live with, adjusted within an hour—and with seemingly little internal conflict—to any new home or environment I dragged him into, and made friends with any and all of the friends or boyfriends I wanted him to make friends with over the years. And while it's true that a handful of veterinarians would have told a very different story on the subject of Homer's alleged good nature (it takes a *lot* for an animal hospital to ban a cat for life, but in his final years Homer distinguished himself by attaining that dubious honor), expecting across-the-board perfection from anybody—much less a cat—is, arguably, to expect too much.

I always think that if cats can be said to belong to certain generations, then Homer—along with his big sisters, Scarlett and

Vashti—were my Gen Xers: three "latchkey kids" with a struggling single mom who worked long hours outside the home and moved them six times in seven years, instilling in them a certain level of flexibility and self-sufficiency. It's possible that this—in combination with his blindness, which forced Homer to learn adaptability from his earliest days just so he could do the everyday things that a "normal" cat could do—forged Homer into an exceptionally tractable, roll-with-the-changes kind of cat.

Clayton and Fanny, on the other hand, are my Millennials. Laurence and I did move with them once when they were just over a year old. But, aside from that early trauma, for the past six years they've lived in the same pleasant, roomy home with a stable couple of work-at-home caretakers who've painstakingly nurtured, probably spoiled, and unquestionably helicopter-parented them to within an inch of their lives.

Clayton and Fanny expect life to bend to their needs and whims, and it never seems to occur to them that it might, in fact, be their whims that ought to bend to the necessities of life. In fairness, it's hard to argue with their conclusions when this has so routinely been how things have worked out for them. At any rate, they are most definitely *not* go-with-the-flow cats. Every hiccup in their lives is an ordeal, even the slightest change in their routines experienced as a profound crisis.

Never is this more apparent than each year in November, when the clocks go back an hour at the end of Daylight Savings Time and all hell breaks loose.

SEASONAL CHANGES ARE SUBTLE in Miami, which is where I'm from originally. I've lived in the Northeast for nearly eighteen years now, and I still experience an almost childlike glee in the beginning of fall. When the leaves change from green to gold and jackets make their first appearances, when it's time to begin stockpiling logs for the fireplace and maybe add a shot of Bailey's to a cup of after-dinner coffee, my heart zings in my chest. And it's not just the change in the outdoor shrubbery's palette, or the sharp drops in temperature, that announces the turning of the year so much more conspicuously up here than back home. Miami's much closer to the Equator than New York, which means that—even with Daylight Savings Time in the summer and its end in the fall—the seasonal differences in sunrise and sunset aren't all that dramatic. At the very height of the summer solstice, sunset in Miami occurs perhaps two hours later than it does at the winter solstice—which is certainly noticeable, but nothing like the five-hour difference we see up north.

The shorter days here are *much* shorter days; and, even without the change in their feeding schedule (trust me, we'll get to the change in their feeding schedule) the effects on Clayton's and Fanny's daily routines still throw them for a loop each year in mid-fall, despite the fact that these very same changes have occurred routinely every single year of their lives.

After eating his breakfast at five a.m., and then sleeping it off for a couple of hours, Clayton likes to station himself in our living room's bay window every morning, to watch the commuters as they stream past our house on their way to catch trains into the city. As the days get shorter and sunrise occurs later, inevitably this daily exodus begins while it's still dark out—and, every year, Clayton seems to take this as a personal affront. He'll be roused from a deep sleep by the sounds of footsteps and people chattering into cell phones outside, at which point Clayton scurry-hops to the window with all the fluster and flurry of a rent-a-cop caught napping on the job. *It's not time yet! What are they doing here so early?!!?* His own internal clock is, after all, synchronized to the movements of the sun, and therefore far more reliable than imperfect human timekeepers with their abstract notions of *this* o'clock and *that* o'clock. If anybody's wrong here, clearly it's everyone else and not my cat, who accordingly takes to scolding these off-time fools for their error, stamping his three little feet back and forth and squeaking an indignant *Meeeeeeee!* at them at the top of his lungs. *Hey! You're not supposed to be walking past our house this early!* Every so often, passersby will pause to stare or point at the furious three-legged black cat in the bay window, while I experience a twinge of the same mortification I might feel if my mother-in-law, wearing curlers and brandishing a rolling pin, were standing in front of our house shouting, *Get off my lawn!*

I wake up so early in part because I like to write first thing in the morning. But with all the hubbub of Clayton's re-education initiatives, I have to wait until well past sun-up before I'm able to recover the quiet I need in order to get the day's writing underway. Fortunately, it only takes a week or two for Clayton to give up as a lost cost his scrupulous efforts to teach humans how to tell time, and I'm left to the serenity of my silent mornings once again.

The high point of Fanny's everyday routine occurs at the opposite end of the day—at night, when I head upstairs to bed. Fanny loves to race up the stairs ahead of me, leap into the middle of the bed, and then pace its perimeter impatiently as I change into my pajamas. Once I'm settled in under the covers and propped up against the pillows, she climbs onto my chest for the half-hour of intense scratching and petting she requires before she'll finally allow me to nod off.

The earlier advent of sunset would undoubtedly tinker with her Circadian rhythms regardless. But the combination of that plus the clocks going back an hour means that, in the early days of November, Fanny will station herself at the bottom of the stairs starting at around seven. (I may not put in as many late nights as I did back in my twenties, but it still seems unkind of Fanny to hasten my aging process by suggesting a seven o'clock bedtime.) Every time I walk past the staircase—on my way to or from the bathroom, or going downstairs to grab something from the kitchen, rather than upstairs to hit the hay—Fanny excitedly darts about halfway up the stairs toward the bedroom before she realizes I'm not following. Upon noting that my decidedly heavier tread can't be heard behind her own dainty feline footsteps, she slowly turns and walks back down to the base of the stairs, her head slumping in disappointment, and turns upon me a look of such round-eyed sadness that it would take someone made of far sterner stuff than I am to avoid feeling like an ogre. *Oh...I guess you weren't looking forward to cuddling with me as much as I was looking forward to cuddling with you.* She then spends the next few hours, until I finally do go up, waiting patiently at the foot of the stairs, assuming an air of wounded martyrdom that really should earn her an Oscar the moment the Academy creates a new category for animal performances.

I can't quite bring myself to pack it in for the night before primetime TV has even started, just to please Fanny. But I do find that I end up dispensing treats and catnip with a much freer hand during those first two weeks in November, while the cats are still adjusting to the end of Daylight Savings Time, than I do at any other point during the year. *I'll give you anything you want—just please, PLEASE stop looking so sad!*

These are little things, perhaps not even worth noticing in and of themselves, although they're joined by innumerable other small adjustments that my cats—and I, by extension—have to make in transitioning from summer to autumn. The sun falls through the windows of my little writing nook differently in the autumn and winter than it does in spring and summer. The stack of my own books that I like to keep on my desk next to my computer—so that I can refer back to them as I write—ends up square in the middle of a sunny patch that isn't there in the warmer months. It makes an ideal sunbathing spot for a couple of cats who like to drowse near their human mom while she works, so naturally I end up moving the books to a less-convenient spot on a shelf behind me, until March, when the sun patterns change once again.

The pretty glass vase and tiny Tiffany lamp that rest behind my laptop computer are now struck directly by the sunlight that only hits them at oblique angles in the summer—which means they throw merry, rainbow colored glares of light against the walls and ceiling. It's lovely to see—or *I* think it is, anyway.

But something about rainbows seems to inspire my cats with a murderous rage. Perhaps, unbeknownst to me, they were traumatized in some way by a rainbow in their early kittenhood? Whatever the reasoning behind it, there's no mistaking their lethal intentions whenever they see one. *Ooh...it's so pretty! WE MUST KILL IT!!!* Fanny and Clayton leap like things possessed all over my desk and my lap as they try *again* and *again*—alas! always without success!—to capture and dismember the refracted sunbeams once and for all. "You guys, it's just *light*," I'll plead, Fanny's hind claws drawing blood from my thighs as she leaps ceiling-ward off of my lap with all her might. "There's nothing *there* for you to catch."

But it always ends the same way—with me hauling out the first-aid kid and then reluctantly removing vase and lamp from my desk altogether, resigning myself to a long winter of overhead lighting once the sun, a little earlier each evening, has gone down.

And yet, I would take the darkness, the scoldings, and the scratches any day of the week and twice on Sunday if only—if only!—doing so would somehow get me off the hook at mealtimes. You might be thinking, *Come on—meals that are only off-schedule by an hour can't be* that *big a deal.* And you would be very, very wrong.

AND IT'S HERE THAT I must present a self-defense of sorts—one that I've repeated ad infinitum to my cats over the years, but the rationality of which they've proven stubbornly immune to. It doesn't help that, in this case, my furry little judge and jury are also my chief prosecutors. Somehow it always seems that I've been tried, convicted of Animal Cruelty in the First Degree, and sentenced to some indefinite period of feline servitude before I've gotten the chance to mount even a rudimentary defense on my own behalf.

But surely you, gentle reader—you who have traveled down so many of the same roads with your own cats as I have with mine—will judge me more kindly. Undoubtedly you'll see that I'm not a monster, not the world's worst cat mom, that I do the very best I can for my cats and every bit as much as any one of you would do for your own, so help me God.

Let the defense show, in the first place, that I feed my cats three meals a day, serving them punctually at five a.m., one p.m., and nine p.m. It should also be noted that, once upon a time in the distant past, Fanny and Clayton were fed at six a.m., two p.m., and ten p.m. But then, in November of 2015, I was working furiously on a self-published sequel to *Homer's Odyssey* that I intended to release in time for the holiday gift-giving season. I didn't have the mental bandwidth to both meet my writing deadline and also tolerate my cats' early-morning chest stompings and mid-afternoon howls of anguish—not to mention the two of them hopping angrily around my desk chair and caterwauling in unison at what they *thought* was their two o'clock lunchtime or ten o'clock dinnertime, but was actually, now that the clocks had gone back, one o'clock or nine o'clock, respectively. So their feeding times went back an hour that November, and an hour back they have remained to this day.

The defense would further like the record to reflect that the majority of cats do *not* receive three meals a day. Most cats live with humans who have sensible real jobs in offices or schools or stores, and who therefore don't fritter away their days scribbling about their cats and posting on social media from home the way I do. How many among us have the luxury of being home often enough to personally serve their cats three delicious, nutritionally balanced meals each and every day? (The prosecution objects on the grounds that "delicious" is a debatable point, as my cats reserve the right to find repulsive even a flavor of food they loved with wild enthusiasm only days earlier. But "nutritionally balanced" is a more objective standard, and the defense will stand by it.)

The scrumptiousness or otherwise of their food notwithstanding (*Yuck—steak and lobster* again?!!? my cats tell me eloquently with their squinted eyes and crinkling noses, before storming off in disgust), Clayton and Fanny pretty much live the pampered lives of cruise ship passengers. They spend their days napping and being shuffled from one extravagant meal to the next. To pass the time, they engage in various recreational activities—rolling around in catnip, frolicking with Da Bird, watching "cat TV," i.e. the birds congregating at the feeders I've attached to the outside of our windows for my cats' entertainment—arranged for them by their attentive cruise director (that would be me) before heading off to eat or nap, or eat and *then* nap, once again. Most of us would pay good money, is what I'm saying, to enjoy for a mere ten days the lifestyle my Clayton and Fanny get to enjoy every blessed day of their charmed lives.

I beseech you, ladies and gentlemen of the jury: are these lavish attentions the actions of a monster?

I know that Scarlett, Vashti, and Homer would have thought they'd been transported to some feline fairyland of flowing abundance if they'd gone to sleep one afternoon, during the first half of their lives, and awakened to find themselves the sole concern of a devoted stay-at-home cat mom, who served them an array of meals in tempting and exotic flavors at three precise intervals every day. When they were Clayton and Fanny's age, I don't think it would have occurred to them that such an extravagance—the stuff of cat daydreams—was even possible.

But Scarlett, Vashti, and Homer weren't raised to quite the same standards or expectations as Clayton and Fanny have been. They got one flavor of dry food and one flavor of moist food for pretty much their entire lives—which only changed once, when Vashti was around eight and developed food allergies, at which point we had to find her a new protein source. Scarlett and Homer ate Vashti's new hypo-allergenic food right along with her, without even a whisper of a complaint, and I doubt very much that it would even have occurred to them that complaining might be warranted.

In fairness to my current cats, though, my first-generation brood did have it easier in some ways. In the ignorant days of my youth—before I knew the health risks associated with a diet made up primarily of dry cat food—I had some down for the cats essentially all the time. "Free grazing" felines, who were able to eat whenever they felt like it regardless of what time it was, wouldn't have found the relatively minor difference of one hour's change forward or backward in their human's schedule particularly earth shaking.

"Earth shaking" seems like the right expression here, because what Clayton and Fanny do to the kitchen every year during the first two weeks of November ends up looking like the aftermath of an earthquake. I'll head downstairs at five in the morning (which my cats now believe is the unreasonably late hour of six) or at one in the afternoon to find that—in the unbearable agony of having to wait *one whole hour* longer for a meal than they think they should have to—my two little miscreants have dumped over their water bowl, shoved their flat food dishes (thoughtfully purchased by me to ensure they're never subjected to the "whisker fatigue" that a deeper bowl might inflict) under the refrigerator, pulled my row of cookbooks down from their shelf above the counter, thrown tchotchkes and tissue boxes and my recipe folder off of the kitchen island, tossed the newspapers we've put aside for recycling all over the floor, spilled out the containers we keep our coffee and pasta in, clawed the roll of paper towels to shreds, and engaged in various other acts of feline vandalism, both large and small.

What? their defiant gazes demand when I finally do make it to the kitchen. *If you weren't so cruel to us, we wouldn't have to resort to this.*

So there I am, before the sun has even come up, faced with at least a half-hour's worth of sponging and mopping and tidying up—and with no greater reward for my efforts than having my two adorable, fuzzy little troublemakers creep into my lap, once their bellies are finally full and satisfied, for a round of cuddles and scritches before they drift off into the day's first purring, contented nap.

It seems like a lot of drama over a mere one-hour discrepancy.

And that's just what happens in the kitchen! If it's lunchtime and I'm working at my desk—teeth gritted as I silently repeat my mantra of, *I will not give in. I will NOT give in!*—they'll send any printed-out manuscripts on the desk next to me skittering merrily into the air, walk across my computer keyboard, nip at my hips and legs, all the while sending up a chorus of alternatively pissed-off and plaintive cries. Or if it's evening and I'm watching TV or reading a book, they'll stand in front of the TV screen, attempt to swat the book from my hands, all while raising such a ruckus of cries and cajolings that it's amazing the neighbors have never complained. Fanny's meows take on a decidedly confrontational edge (*J'accuse!*), while Clayton opts for pathos. *Doncha love us anymore, mom?* his sad, sad string of mews—eventually fading in volume as the weakness of starvation (because of an hour! *one* hour!)—begins to set in.

I love my cats—I do! I love them like crazy!—and I would do anything in the world for them. Surely—*surely*—you, my readers, can see that.

But I won't knuckle under on this one. I won't do it. I won't give them lunch at noon, or start getting up at four a.m. to feed them breakfast. Because where would it end? This year's four a.m. would become next year's three a.m. once the clocks go back again, and then the following year's two a.m. Eventually I'd be getting up to feed them breakfast *literally* before I'd gone to bed the night before!

The madness has to stop somewhere! *Somebody* has to hold the line, to keep our lives from descending into the chaos that would reign if my two little would-be dictators had their druthers!

And if these are the actions of an ogre, ladies and gentlemen of the jury, then what can I say? Condemn me if you must and hang me high.

But know as you do so that I'm taking this stand not only on my own behalf, but for all of you as well. Undoubtedly some of you have fought this same fight and thought that you were fighting it alone. Know, then, that you have an ally in me—someone who will stand by your side and go to the mat for you as we battle against this one, just this *one,* encroachment on our lives and liberties by the fuzzy feline overlords to whom we've given so much of ourselves already. Is one measly hour of sleep in the morning really so much to ask? If the answer is no, and I believe that it is, then we must stand together—firm and united—if we're ever to enter the golden Promised Land of adequate sleep. And I will mount that hangman's scaffold, brothers and sisters, with my head held high, knowing the glory of the cause for which I fight.

It is a far, far better thing that I do, than I have ever done; it is a far, far better rest that I go to (one blissfully uninterrupted by the yowling of hungry cats) than I have ever known.

And, with that, the defense rests.

IT'S POSSIBLE THAT I'VE allowed myself to get a *weeeeee* bit carried away (ahem). Truth be told, I've never been a huge fan of Daylight Savings Time—or, at least, the ending of Daylight Savings Time, when the clocks go back an hour. It's nice in theory to get an extra hour on a Sunday, but that extra hour comes in the middle of the night. What usually happens is that my body wakes me up at what it thinks is five a.m., but is now actually four, and I lie there for an hour trying my best to ignore my cats' desperate pleas for breakfast and willing myself to fall back asleep, so as to adjust to the new schedule as quickly as possible. I then spend the rest of the day, and the next few days, in a bit of a daze because, y'know, I've been up since *four o'clock a.m.*—which is a tad on the early side, even for me.

Apparently, I'm not alone in wishing that the clocks never had to go backward. The American Academy of Sleep Medicine reports that "falling back" can cause drowsiness for weeks after the change, and there's even been some research that's tied it to an increase in traffic accidents and heart attacks. The costs, both human and feline, of this arbitrary change to everybody's schedule are mounting up.

Recently I read that voters in California, in the last election, had overwhelmingly supported Proposition 7, which would make Daylight Savings Time permanent. There would be one last spring forward, after which the great state of California would never fall back again. If the ballot measure ends up getting the approval of the state congress and clearing various bureaucratic hurdles, the people of California will have one extra hour of sunshine—with which to enjoy some additional sunbathing, tend their gardens, and engage in other outdoor activities—all year round.

More importantly, the cat moms and dads of California will never again be awakened at ungodly early hours by the plaintive cries of put-upon cats who, when you get right down to it, only want what everybody wants—meals that are served reliably on schedule. Never again will they have their kitchens and desks trashed by fussy felines expressing distress in the only way cats know how. Peace and serenity will reign between cats and humans—or, at least, it will until the next time somebody decides to change the brand of their cats' litter, or to move a beloved kitty condo from one window to another, at which point the battle will begin anew.

There's an obvious wisdom in all this, to which I can add only one thing:

California, here I come.

Just BeClaws

THERE'S A CAT IN our neighborhood who I've become somewhat obsessed with. His name is Oliver, and he's a gorgeous, fluffy tuxedo cat with huge green eyes (that are, rather adorably, a teensy bit crossed) and a glorious black bottle-brush tail. He's an indoor/outdoor cat who appears to belong to the people who live right across the street from us, although the scuttlebutt on the block is that, while only one house takes him in at night, there are two families that feed him.

Oliver is perhaps best described as a cat of ambivalent desires. I see him through the front windows of my home as he forlornly runs after anyone who talks to him, or even so much as looks at him, begging for attention. The softest beckoning *pss-pss-pss* sound from me will bring him flying across the street and all the way up the steep flight of stairs leading to my front door, where Oliver will immediately begin cavorting about my ankles and shins in a cat's age-old *pleeeeeeeeease pet me!* dance. If I lower my hand, he'll rise halfway up on his hind legs to thrust the top of his head eagerly into it, purring to beat the band.

The first couple of weeks we were here, it would break my heart to see Oliver chasing hopefully after first one passerby, then another, and be ignored nearly every single time. What kind of neighborhood had I moved into, I wondered? What kind of people would so callously brush off a love-starved cat who was all but abjectly pleading for the merest scrap of affection? Unable to bear it, I finally headed out one afternoon armed with a bag of salmon-flavored Greenies and a determination to bestow upon this neglected kitty some of the cuddles he so clearly craved.

I found Oliver in our back yard, as it happened, where he'd managed to corner a squirrel, despite the forewarning provided by the pink belled collar he wears. The rattle of the treats bag drew his attention away from the beleaguered squirrel and he raced over to me, but he ignored the treats I sprinkled liberally onto our back deck. I was touched to see that it apparently wasn't the treats at all that had interested him, but rather *me*, myself, that had brought him across the yard.

As Oliver rubbed furiously around my ankles, I crouched down to pet him, which he seemed to enjoy enthusiastically for about thirty seconds or so. And then, without warning, he let out an enraged hiss and slashed furiously at my bare legs with his claws. Figuring I'd inadvertently startled him or hit a sensitive spot—and not wanting to alarm him any further—I remained hunkered down on my ankles, slowly withdrew my hand, and waited quietly until Oliver approached me again. He did so while also doing everything in a cat's power—via rubbing, purring, and insistent head bonks—to indicate, *I want petting NOW!*

It pains me (literally) to report that this second attempt ended almost exactly the way the first one had, except that this time Oliver's claws landed in a slightly different spot. By the time I finally abandoned the effort and, sadder but wiser, headed back inside, my legs looked like two blood-streaked scratching posts. It occurred to me that I might have been unfair in my original assessment of my neighbors' callousness—and, in fact, I would later confirm that Oliver was notorious for blocks around for precisely this MO.

It's a pattern that's repeated itself numerous times in the months since then. Sometimes it's my hands and arms that take the worst abuse, sometimes my shins and knees—but, inevitably, the essential result is always the same. The scratchings are unpleasant, but I am, perhaps, stupid in my desire to help this cat overcome whatever emotional block it is that makes him chase away the very affection he's clearly so desperate for. For a cat to crave love so profoundly, yet never attain it, strikes me as an unbearable tragedy—and what are we on this earth for if not, at least in part, to rewrite real life's tragedies with happy endings?

Laurence doesn't take quite so philosophical a view of the situation, and the last time I came in with ribbons of blood running down my legs, heading for the medicine chest and a tube of Neosporin, he was downright furious.

"Leave that cat alone!" he shouted. "He obviously wants to be left alone."

"But he *doesn't*," I insisted. "You see how he begs for attention. He won't spook so easily once he knows there's someone he's safe with."

"You have no idea what you're doing," Laurence informed me. "You're not a professional."

"I mean...I'm *kind* of a professional," I said. "It says so right on our tax return." Which is true. Every year, when we file our paperwork with the IRS, in the blank space where it asks for my occupation, our accountant always writes in *Cat Author/Expert*.

"You know what I mean," Laurence grumbled, and I immediately retorted, "No, I *don't* know what you mean," and by that point we'd so clearly devolved into one of those *Are not!/Am so!* arguments that never reach any kind of satisfying resolution, it seemed best to discontinue the conversation altogether.

Laurence and I will never see eye to eye on this one. He sees Oliver as a lost cause. I, however, refuse to give up hope.

And I've got the scabby, clawed-up shins to prove it.

JUST REMEMBER, MY MOTHER used to tell my sister and me, *skin grows back. Clothing and furniture don't.*

This was always said in reference to our dogs, some of whom over the years combined a propensity for jumping up on you enthusiastically with a reluctance to allow their claws to be trimmed—which was especially problematic, say, late in the life of a larger dog, when poor balance, combined with those other two factors, ultimately created a situation wherein *something* was going to end up with claw marks. It was only a question of what, specifically, that something would be. My mother's point was that we should try to angle our jumping dogs' claw-y fervor so that our arms and legs—rather than our clothes or nearby furniture—took the brunt of it.

Parents had different philosophies about such things back then than the "helicopter" parents of today.

All of our dogs were rescues, and most of them came to us from abusive situations—which meant that we had more than our fair share of dogs who, in working through their understandable anxiety, would sometimes claw up furniture or rugs. My mother, who did love our dogs dearly, would nevertheless occasionally lament that she couldn't fix up our house the way she'd *really* like to, if only circumstances had been permitting. *If only we didn't have anxious dogs*, is what she meant. It was my first inculcation into one of the world's great truths: that everything in life is a tradeoff.

Probably just about everybody has some idea of a Dream Room that they'd like to live in someday—and a few lucky people even get the chance to see that dream become a reality. Sometimes, when watching some Netflix show about people building their dream home in, say, an abandoned grain silo or former nuclear bunker, I'll admit that I've wept unabashedly at seeing those lucky, lucky people at the end of the hour, now in glorious possession of a sun-soaked home library in what used to be a medieval bell tower, or an immaculately appointed living room sprawling across a space once occupied by a 1920s fire station.

My own conception of the Dream Room I aspire to live in will vary depending upon my mood or state of mind. When feeling particularly stressed out, I'll imagine the sort of Mediterranean living room you see in pictures of Greece—all white walls, white upholstery, tons of sunlight, and the occasional "pop" of aqua-marine blue in a throw pillow or wall hanging. In the depths of winter, I'm apt to imagine a sort of English Library living room, with low beamed ceilings, oaken bookcases, well-worn Oriental rugs, comfortable furniture in muted earth tones, and an old stone hearth. If I'm feeling homesick for Miami, the Dream Room I imagine has Spanish influences in its tall windows, high dark-wood ceilings, golden stucco walls, and jewel-tone upholstery.

I've never lived in a room remotely like any of these, and at a certain point in life—and deep into one's forties is probably as good a time as any—I've had to acknowledge that I probably never will. My daydreams may conjure gilded palaces in the air, but my real life is less a showcase for Nice Things and is instead rather more sensibly accessorized by sturdy, sensible, mid-priced furniture—the kind that looks nice *enough*, particularly when accented by cute little throw pillows and suchlike, but that's also designed to withstand years of abuse (or love, depending upon your perspective) without showing too much wear and tear.

Some of this is the result of the inexorable realities of money and circumstances. (It seems to me, for example, the I can live in the Northeast, and I can live in a Greek-influenced Mediterranean-style home, but very likely I can't do both of these things at the same time.) But primarily it comes down to certain choices I've made over the years—choices that I have absolutely zero regrets over, but which, despite my satisfaction with them, inevitably come with consequences.

I'm referring, of course, to the choice I made some twenty-five years ago to become a "cat mom."

I can already hear the protests exclaiming that there are any number of alternatives and solutions available to someone who's determined to make a happy home with both cats on the one hand and furnishings swathed in silks, suede, and antique wood on the other. Frequent claw trimmings, Soft Paws gel caps, ubiquitous scratching posts (which, it's worth noting, are present in abundance in my home), and so on. I've read all the same articles and blogs and expert commentary that everybody else has read, and have followed all the advice that's seemed practicable over the years. But things in life aren't always as straightforward as they're made to seem in self-help guides and advice columns. (This, by the way, is another one of the world's great truths.)

Homer, for example, always had a morbid fear of having his claws trimmed, which intensified, rather than diminishing, over the years. By the time he'd turned ten, you were pretty much taking your life in your hands if you so much as brushed one of Homer's talons with your finger, much less attempted to trim it—a precept that applied not just to hapless groomers and vet techs, but even to me, the person he trusted most. I always understood, though, that the world is an uncertain and often dangerous-seeming place to a little blind cat; if Homer felt safer moving through life secure in the knowledge that he had ten tiny switchblades attached to the ends of his paws, who was I to take that away from him?

But Homer's claws were far more to him than just his primary weapons of defense or offense. In encountering some new object, for example, whose height Homer was unsure of, he was more apt—at least at first—to attempt scaling it rather than leaping to the top of it, in which case his claws were less like tiny switchblades and more like little pickaxes that helped him scale even the most intimidating of heights. It sometimes seemed to me that Homer's claws were, to him, what my driver's license had been to me when I turned sixteen—something that ensured him both independence and mobility, the freedom to go wherever his fancy might take him. To shear Homer's claws would, therefore, be to rob him of some portion of that spirited independence, which he so fiercely loved and which I so fiercely loved him for.

And it would hardly be reasonable to my other two cats to keep *their* claws trimmed down while allowing Homer's to sharpen until they were practically hypodermic needles—particularly as everybody got older and crankier and more apt to swipe at each other in irritation from time to time. Allowing Homer to refine his claws into razor-sharp points on our various scratching posts while blunting Vashti's and Scarlett's with claw-trimmers would have been tantamount to creating a one-sided arms race in my home—one that would have left Vashti and Scarlett virtually defenseless. It would have upset the entire balance of power—and, as anybody with multiple cats knows, a peaceful group dynamic is a hard-won thing, and one that shouldn't be tampered with.

But, naturally, it wasn't primarily upon each other that my cats exercised their claws. Furniture and human skin bore the brunt of it. I told myself, as I bade tearful farewells to things over the years—to a red velvet loveseat I'd picked up for a song at a moving sale, and that I'd loved with an unreasonable love; to the leather recliner that Laurence had been living with for more than a decade when the four of us moved in with him, and which lasted exactly six months, once subjected to Vashti's tender mercies, before one side of it was stripped all the way down to its wooden frame—that I'd rather have one Homer and one Vashti than a thousand velvet loveseats and leather chairs. There was a life of having Nice Things on the one hand, and then there was having the Good Things in life, which were infinitely more important, on the other—Good Things like love and laughter and the daily miracle of a warm, fuzzy (and, in the case of *my* cats, heavily armed) little critter trusting you enough to fall asleep peacefully on your lap.

There was no question on which side of the equation I placed the cats I loved.

And what did it matter if it was occasionally my skin that got the worst of it? What did it signify if every spirited game of "wiggling fingers under the bedsheets" was apt to leave a days-long reminder of long red welts on the backs of my hands, or if I sometimes—after the brutal slog of bundling Homer into his carrier for a vet's visit—had to slather my wrists in honey for a week in order to speed up the healing process? After all, as my mother reminded me all those years ago, skin does eventually grow back.

That was back in the old days, but even today, things aren't much different. My cat Fanny, ballerina that she is, will leap nimbly from the floor to the top of the mantelpiece, and from the mantelpiece to the top of a seven-foot bookcase, with graceful ease. My three-legged Clayton, however, bless his furry little heart, isn't much of a jumper—which is only to be expected of a cat who has only one hind leg. Clayton works frantically to keep up with his beloved Fanny, and while he doesn't quite succeed in going *everywhere* that Fanny can get to, his ability to climb gets him a good part of the way—and, naturally, climbing requires claws. Nothing breaks my heart more than to see Clayton, fresh from a claw-trimming, trying desperately to huff and puff his way up the side of the couch or the bed, only to fall off helplessly and land on his back, his three legs and pudgy little tummy splayed upward as he turns upon me a look of bewildered betrayal. *Why? Why did you do this to me?!*

(As a side note, it always mystifies me as to *how* it is that Clayton and Fanny can be litter-mates—who eat the exact same food in the exact same quantities every single day—and yet Fanny is slender as a gymnast while Clayton is a mushy little pudge-boy. Genetics are a wacky thing.)

And so, once again, when selecting a new couch for our new home a few months ago, I opted for a sofa swathed in an inexpensive-yet-sturdy gray material that seemed unlikely to show much in the way of claw marks—at least not for the first few years. And, this time around, we opted for a modestly priced metal coffee table to accompany it. We have a small, wooden magazine rack next to the couch, but we mostly keep our magazines in less convenient, tougher-to-get-to spots up out of the cats' reach—Clayton being inordinately fond of shredding anything paper. There's very little more frustrating than coming to the end of one of those loooooooooong, four-thousand-word *New Yorker* articles, only to find that a furry miscreant has beaten you to the punch and made confetti out of the last few paragraphs. Hardcover books with paper dustjackets live on the very top shelves of our bookcase, where Clayton can't reach at all and where even Fanny would find it difficult to exercise her scratching impulses without some sort of assistance. We have enough cat scratchers, scratching posts, claw-able cat beds, and sisal-roped climbing cat towers in our house for ten felines or more, but still—there's no point in placing unnecessary temptation in our cats' paths.

Fanny and Clayton are, like most felines, just as engaged by games like "wiggling fingers under the bedsheets" or "catch mom's ankles as she walks by" as my first generation of cats were. Clayton particularly likes to blissfully knead his claws into my stomach, or dig them firmly into the skin of my arms (so as to hug me close) as he lies contentedly on my lap. In the winter months, when my skin is paler, the daily evidence of my cats' love for me on my hands, ankles, and torso is particularly striking (although, fortunately for me, these cats are FAR easier to wrangle into their carriers than my first three cats were).

Sometimes, my cats will love me hardest just before I'm scheduled to do a reading and book signing—and, when someone is standing one foot away from you while you sign a book for them, your scratched and scabby signing hand is about as conspicuous as it's ever going to be. This always provoke a certain amount of consternation in me, as I diligently apply healing balms and unguents to various exposed parts of my body, not wanting to appear unsightly to people who've paid me the incredible honor of traveling to a shelter or bookstore just to meet me.

Occasionally I wonder, though, why I worry about it so much. What, after all, could a few stray claw marks on the person of a well-known cat writer be, if not badges of authenticity?

I VISITED A NEW Jersey no-kill cat shelter a while back to do a reading, arriving an hour before the reading was scheduled so that a veteran staffer could give me a tour and introduce me to some of the kitties. She was wearing a long-sleeved tee and had pushed the sleeves up to her elbow, revealing forearms that were literally battle-scarred—a veritable topographical map of long white lines that had accrued over more than a decade of being a dedicated cat rescuer. Most of the claw marks and scars were long-since healed, and they crisscrossed her arms from the backs of her hands all the way up to her elbows with reminders of yesteryear's rescue cats.

I've visited hundreds of shelters over the past decade, and I've met thousands of rescuers. But I couldn't remember ever having seen one who carried such clear visual evidence of her calling—who'd endured more for the sake of spaying and neutering ferals, or patiently helping an anxious cat adjust to life in a shelter environment. They were the arms of someone who refused to give up on any cat, even when those cats did their worst. And I could tell, by the enthusiastic greetings she got from nearly every cat in all of the cage-free "kitty dormitories" we visited, that her persistence had paid off. As a particularly affectionate ginger leapt into her arms by way of greeting, I couldn't help gesturing to her arms and noting, "I guess they're not always this friendly at first." But she just beamed at me and said, "Some of these are love marks, too."

"Don't let them love you to death," I said wryly, and the staffer laughed cheerfully in response—acknowledging another of the world's great truths: that if love sometimes makes us do strange things, it just as often shows itself in strange ways.

Back when I lived in Miami, my then-boyfriend Jorge's mother, Maggie, fed a colony of feral cats that lived in the woods near her home. Most of the cats were so shy that they'd duck back into the trees if they so much as caught a glimpse of you, but there was among them an enormous and friendly tom who Jorge's mother had named Pinto.

Pinto was a stocky gray tabby who Maggie had had neutered, and he was skittish as a wild animal for the first few months after returning to his colony. Over time, however—and after a months-long course of steady feedings accompanied by no loud noises or sudden movements—he became bolder and friendlier. We soon discovered that—for as large as he was and as fierce as he looked (particularly with his one lopped ear)—Pinto was nothing more than a big old lap cat, although he only ever warmed to Maggie and to me. When Jorge and I visited his parents' home on weekends for Sunday brunch, I would spend long hours sitting cross-legged on the ground of their front porch with Pinto's bulk flopped across my lap, purring like a racecar engine as I scratched his back and stroked his head and rubbed beneath his chin while his eyes closed in ecstasy.

Inevitably, of course—and usually long before he was ready—I would eventually have to dislodge Pinto and head back inside. I know that Jorge's parents had a made a brief, abortive attempt at converting Pinto into a house cat, but the experience of bringing Pinto inside had been traumatic enough for all concerned that it wasn't attempted again until an approaching hurricane some months later forced the matter.

But, at that time, going inside meant leaving Pinto behind—something that didn't please Pinto at all. In an effort to stop me, he would rear up and grab at my arms and legs with his claws extended, ruthlessly digging all of those claws into me in an attempt to hold onto me and force me to remain outside with him. And, so, my love sessions with this giant feral kitty who had an even bigger heart—whose manners were, perhaps, not all that they should have been (and what else could you fairly expect from a semi-wild cat?)—would almost always end with a bloody scratch-mark or two. That Pinto loved me, I never doubted. Perhaps he didn't quite love me to death, but he certainly wasn't shy about leaving evidence of his love behind.

I thought about Pinto just the other day while attempting, once again, to pet Oliver on the front steps of my house. As per usual, I came back into the house scratched and bloodied for my troubles. But this time Oliver hadn't scratched me while I was petting him. This time, like Pinto, he didn't scratch me at all until I *stopped* petting him and prepared to head inside, when he reared up on his hind legs and wrapped himself around me with all his might, refusing to let me go.

Furtively sneaking into the house and up to the bathroom medicine chest—with its bandages and Neosporin—before Laurence could notice me, I couldn't help but smile and feel pleased as I tended to this latest round of claw-inflicted wounds.

Oliver and I were definitely making progress.

The Bells

By the time I adopted Fanny and Clayton, it had been nearly fifteen years since I'd lived with a kitten. And although my little feline family had felt complete—more than complete—once I'd adopted Homer all those years ago, there had always been a part of me that had longed for the tiny, adorable, curious and obstinate, rough-and-tumble sweetness of a kitten. Since *Homer's Odyssey* had been published a few years earlier, I'd visited more cat shelters in far-flung corners of the country than I could count—and, always, there were kittens in need of homes who I'd cradled and cuddled close and sighed over, before reluctantly returning them back to their caretakers. Fortunately, I'd never followed through on the mad impulse I occasionally felt to simply stuff a kitten into my handbag and stroll out nonchalantly. (*My purse isn't meowing! Maybe* your *purse is meowing!*) But the temptation was a sore one, and Laurence always heaved a barely concealed sigh of relief each time I returned from a shelter visit in possession of no larger number of cats than I'd left home with.

Nevertheless, when Homer suddenly found himself an only cat after the passing of Scarlett—a distinction he'd never wanted and clearly was not enjoying—my first thought had been to adopt some nice, mellow, middle-aged cat as a companion for him. Homer was fifteen by then, after all. A rambunctious kitten would almost certainly require more energy on Homer's part than he seemed able to spare these days.

Homer's obvious grief after we lost Scarlett—the way he dragged himself, like an old man with stiff joints, through our home; the listless manner in which he gave some favored toy a cursory bat with his paw before slinking disconsolately away from it—had been difficult to see, and his sadness had deepened and extended my own. Even four months later, it was impossible to be happy when Homer was unhappy, to feel that I was moving past my grief when Homer so clearly was unable to move past his. Laurence, on more than one occasion, observed that, "This has become a sad house," and he spoke the truth.

And, while it arguably shouldn't have mattered, Homer's grief was made all the more difficult for me to bear by my rock-solid certainty that Scarlett herself—had she wound up as the last cat standing rather than Homer—would have greeted the return of her "only child" status, after so many years of sharing her home with two other cats she'd never wanted, with unabashed glee. *Don't be sad for Scarlett,* I wanted to yell at Homer sometimes. *She wouldn't have been sad for you!* But grief, like all emotions, rarely obeys strict logic, and that sort of reasoning—born as much from my own fear for Homer's health and wellbeing as anything else—almost certainly wouldn't have mattered much to a human mourner, much less a feline one.

Vashti and Scarlett may have gone far out of their way to exclude and avoid Homer as much as possible back in the old days, but they'd nevertheless formed a crucial component of his daily social life. With a seemingly deliberate obliviousness, he had pursued the two of them—trying to engage them in play or long, companionable naps together—every day for fifteen years. Now there was nobody for Homer to play or socialize with, except for a mom who'd never be as good at doing cat things as that cattiest of all possible cats, my Scarlett, had been.

I wasn't sure how Homer would react to having to get used to a new cat for the very first time in his life. Homer, himself, had been my last "new cat." But, after four months of unsuccessful attempts to get Homer out of his funk and coax him back into the spirited playfulness that had once been his trademark, I was both desperate and fresh out of other ideas.

Neither of the mellow, middle-aged cats I'd agreed to foster, however, in the hopes of finding a new companion for Homer, had proved to be a match personality-wise. They'd gone on to forever homes of their own, and in their wake I was left with the growing realization that a kitten, despite my reservations, was probably the best way to go. I was extraordinarily reluctant to add even an additional particle of unhappiness to Homer's already too-heavy burden by forcing upon him the necessity of adjusting himself to a new cat's quirks, preferences, or temperament. A kitten, on the other hand, would be the one to adjust to Homer's personality and preferences—Homer would be the reigning "big cat" of our home—without expecting any similar effort on Homer's part.

It also stood to reason that, if I were going to adopt *one* kitten to be a companion to Homer, then in reality I'd have to adopt *two*—so they could bounce and bandy and tear around our home with each other, hopefully without pestering Homer too much if his own enthusiasm was more limited than theirs.

And so it was that, after fifteen kitten-free years—during which I'd never entirely gotten over my desire to add a new kitten to our household—I suddenly found myself preparing to adopt not just one, but two new kittens at the same time.

So EXCITED AND RESTLESS was I the night before I was due to receive these kittens who were destined (I hoped!) to save Homer from his overwhelming sorrow—so eager with anticipation during the long train ride from Manhattan down to Trenton, NJ, where I was to collect them from a rescue group called Furrever Friends—and so thoroughly prepared was I to adore them, there was probably very little they could have done to disappoint me. Their very kitten-ness was all I asked for at that point, knowing full well that their actual personalities would ultimately be something of a crap shoot. Even if they turned out to be withdrawn or aloof kittens—like Scarlett herself had been—who shunned Homer, I told myself that simply being able to hear them frolicking about in our home, the return of life and activity to what had become a deathly silent apartment, would surely do Homer some good.

Nevertheless, Clayton and Fanny managed to wildly exceed these very modest expectations.

Even with all of a mom's prejudice, I would never suggest that Clayton and Fanny were perfect cats. (Nor would I want them to be—as any cat lover knows, our cats' imperfections are what make them so very loveable.) But the trait that made them perfect for us—the perfect kittens, or so I thought initially, to bring Homer back to himself—was on full display from that very first day when they came to live with us at just under twelve weeks of age.

Whatever their faults and foibles may be, Fanny and Clayton are cats who were very clearly made for love. Without question, they're two of the most physically affectionate cats I've ever seen. Clayton warms to new people instantly, while Fanny, being shyer, takes a bit longer to feel comfortable around newcomers. But they both seem pre-programmed to like or love everybody they meet, and they express their likings in the most demonstrative ways possible—with head bonks, lap jumps, intense cuddling sessions played out to the accompaniment of diesel-engine purrs. They groom each other to a high gloss every day and attempt to do the same for Laurence and me—the loving care expressed by the ritual of it seeming to compel them to keep going regardless of the fact that Laurence and I, despite our cats' best efforts, are unable to achieve anything like their level of shiny sleekness without the application of copious quantities of human-grade grooming products. If we're walking through the house, it's usually with at least one cat rubbing lovingly against our ankles, and rarely do we sit down on the couch or in a desk chair without one or the other of them immediately leaping onto our legs to join us. If we're busy or otherwise not well situated for lap time, then Clayton and Fanny are almost certain to be found curled up with each other, unable to resist the constant impulse to "love on" someone or something else, even in their sleep. When visitors spend the night in our guest room, they're never permitted to spend the night alone, nor even to engage in bedtime preparations without at least one of our cats keeping them company to make sure they aren't lonesome. (Fanny is particularly fond of sitting raptly at the feet of female guests while they perform complicated nighttime beauty rituals.)

It was obvious that the two of them had been very well loved by the foster mom who'd had them for the first three months of their life; they could never have been so outgoing and confident in their displays of affection if they hadn't come to believe that their little demonstrations would be reciprocated. Their intense love for each other was equally obvious—and it must have seemed to them as natural as breathing to extend their small circle of two wide enough to include others as well.

Of course Clayton and Fanny were fascinated by Homer—always on the smaller side by adult-cat standards, but still the biggest cat our two new kittens had ever seen—right from the start. With eager affection—and within 24 hours of having been released from our guest bedroom for the first time—the kittens progressed almost immediately from following Homer around in silent, respectful enthrallment to trying to include him in their playtimes and grooming sessions and catnap cuddle piles. They batted their toys at Homer's paws, hoping he might bat the toys back. If they came upon Homer in the act of bathing himself, they crawled eagerly atop him, ready to "help" by applying their own tiny tongues to the task. And the sight of Homer attempting to snooze by himself struck them as a tragedy in need of immediate remedy. *Taking a nap, Homer? Howsabout we all curl up together!*

That Homer might not be receptive to these advances—that he might find them bewildering and off-putting—was something that would never have occurred unaided to Fanny and Clayton (especially Clayton—who, to this day, lives firm in the belief that everybody loves him instantly). It was a lesson that Homer, armed with raised paw and warning hiss, had to teach them almost from scratch.

Poor Homer—not only an old man by this time, but also occasionally a crotchety one—had always been an intensely affectionate cat himself. But that was primarily with people. Homer's sole experience with other cats had been with two older sisters who'd never voluntarily touched him or allowed themselves to be touched by him without his having to chase them down first. No other cat had ever wanted to groom Homer with a gently rasping tongue, or cuddle with him as they slept, or follow Homer from room to room in the hopes that *he* might play with *them*.

In a sense, Clayton and Fanny were perfectly suited to give Homer something he'd never had, but had surely always wanted. And yet, after all this time, to suddenly be on the receiving end of *so much* cat-on-cat love was something that Homer had never imagined for himself. It was an unexpected windfall to brighten his golden years, to be sure—but Homer was as unprepared to manage this startling embarrassment of riches as someone living in poverty is to suddenly command millions of dollars, should they happen to buy a winning lottery ticket.

This unprecedented orgy of attention was bewildering for Homer—a bewilderment compounded by the fact that, being blind, of course he could never *see* the kittens coming. It was inevitably disquieting, for example, for Homer to awaken abruptly from a deep sleep, with no advance warning whatsoever, because a small plastic mouse—which Clayton had dragged over to maul while leaning convivially against the warmth of Homer's flank—had been dumped unceremoniously on his head. (*Wanna chew up this mouse with me, Homer?*) Or to be eating from his food bowl, minding his own business, and suddenly find Fanny's tiny tush, seemingly materializing from out of nowhere, pushed solicitously against his snout. (Fanny's...fanny...is a vivid hot pink that's a tad startling against the jet black of her fur, and she takes great pride in showing it off.)

Homer's hearing had always been uncannily sharp. But it was still nearly impossible for him to hear the kittens approaching on their velvety-soft kitten paws. Even Clayton's three-legged little hop was essentially inaudible—at least until he'd landed square across Homer's belly (and then—believe me—we heard it!). Homer never knew when the newest affectionate attack would come, and, after only a few days, the wear and tear of having to live in a constant state of anticipation was taking its toll. While it was true that Homer began to seem more active and less depressed than he had been, it was the activity of anxiety that primarily propelled him now—a constant state of high alert as he tried to anticipate when and from what direction the newest onslaught would be launched. I'd have been apt to describe the situation by saying that Homer now slept with one eye open, if only Homer'd had eyes. But, even in sleep—or what was passing for Homer's sleep these days—his ears were always up and alert, and he now reposed in a sort of defensive crouch, rather than curled up in the tight little ball that had always indicated he felt completely comfortable and at ease.

This wasn't the change in Homer that I'd been hoping to affect by bringing Clayton and Fanny into his life. I knew that things would be easier for Homer if only I were able to devise some sort of early-warning system that would give him a heads-up that a kitten was approaching well before that kitten was actually on top of him.

I'm embarrassed to admit that the very obvious solution to this problem took me nearly three days to come up with. It finally hit me at six o'clock in the morning over coffee one sunny Wednesday, and that very afternoon I walked down to our local pet store and came home with two kitten-sized, breakaway belled collars—a blue one for Clayton, and a pink one for Fanny.

CONTRARY TO A COMMONLY held belief, writing *Homer's Odyssey* has not made me an expert on cats in general, nor on any cats specifically other than my own—and, even when it comes to my own cats, they still manage to surprise me on occasion.

I actually didn't know Fanny and Clayton very well at that point; we'd barely been living together for a week, after all. Still, I knew enough about cats to surmise that getting my kittens into belled collars would likely be a wee bit more complicated than simply fastening the collars onto them one day and letting everything run smoothly from there.

According to an article that I'd read online, the key was to get the kittens used to the collars over a period of days before I attempted actually putting the collars on them. The first step was to gently lay the collars across the backs of the kittens' necks without trying to fasten them, to get Clayton and Fanny used to the collars' weight and sound. *Seems easy enough,* I thought. *How hard could it be?*

Armed with what seemed like a refreshingly simple-to-execute plan of attack, I headed to the living room, belled collars in hand, and shook them until they rang out with an engaging jingle. "Heyyyyyy, kitties," I called, in the tempting tone I usually used when dispensing treats. "Look what I've got. Look what *I've* got, kitties!"

Three-legged Clayton, never one to resist a summoning, came hippity-hopping over first and gave the collars an amiable sniff, followed a moment later by Fanny. Homer had given up playing with any of his many belled toys after we'd lost Scarlett, but from his spot on the couch across the room, he raised his head with mild interest upon hearing the collars' tinkle. Fanny and Clayton continued to give the collars a good going over with their tiny black noses while I stroked their backs reassuringly.

"Now we're just going to gently lay the collars across you, like so..." I told the kittens in a soothing voice, and very carefully draped the collars along the backs of their necks, making no further attempt to fasten them on.

I hadn't expected Clayton and Fanny to *love* the collars, exactly—or even to tolerate them particularly well at first. But I was still unprepared for the vehemence of their reaction, which swiftly went from an interested, *Hmmmm...what are these belled things?* to, *GOOD GOD—SHE'S PUTTING THOSE BELLED THINGS ON TOP OF US!!!* Their little backs arched and puffed, and—apparently firm in the belief that I had just, inexplicably, attempted to murder them—their seven little paws scuttled for purchase on the slippery hardwood floor before the kittens finally skittered off to plunge themselves safely beneath the bed. Clayton was the first to creep out of hiding about a half-hour later (*I guess you weren't* really *trying to kill me,* his forgiving head-bonk conceded), but I wouldn't see Fanny again for a good five hours.

"What's all *that* about?" Laurence inquired, walking into the living room just in time to see Clayton and Fanny dart past his ankles, by all indications in fear for their very lives.

"I think the new guys might be a *wee* bit skittish," I told him drily.

It wasn't much smoother going over the next few days. Every time I approached the kittens with the collars, they reacted as if they were a couple of teenaged girls in a horror movie and I was a crazed spree killer chasing after them with a butcher knife. This was despite my working fun things like treats, catnip, and even a sprinkling of new toys into the routine as I tried with increasing desperation to get them to—at the very least—accept having the belled collars in the general vicinity of their necks. "It's just a collar, you guys," I'd call after their rapidly retreating backsides—alas, to no avail. "A *collar!* It can't *possibly* hurt you!" And then, once I'd found myself alone again, I'd mutter under my breath, *Aye yi yi...*

As it turned out, it was Homer himself who salvaged the situation. The sounds of something belled ringing out—almost immediately followed by the additional clamor of Clayton and Fanny fleeing in terror—finally piqued Homer's curiosity enough that, for the first time in months, he would creep over from the couch to see what all the fuss was about. The kittens having cleared the scene, I'd then dangle the belled collars in front of Homer for his amusement—they should still serve *some* useful purpose, I thought—and he'd bat them around with increasing liveliness as the days went by.

I knew I was making progress when, on the third or fourth day, Clayton dared to peek around the corner from the hallway into the living room long enough to observe Homer playing with one of the belled collars. Anything that Homer was intrigued by was also intriguing to Clayton, and soon enough the two of them were batting one of the collars back and forth between them on the ground—Homer with a wariness that bordered on reluctance at the prospect of engaging directly with one of these new cats, and Clayton with wild enthusiasm that Homer had *finally* consented to play with him, if only a little. Homer would swipe at one of the collars in a languid, almost random fashion, and Clayton's little rump and thick, stocky tail would rise straight up in the air as he scampered from side to side, looking for the exact right angle from which to bat the collar back in Homer's direction. It was almost as if he thought he could inject some of his own excitement for this game into Homer, if only he were excited enough about it.

By the end of a week, even Fanny was getting in on the action, and the kittens were engrossed enough in playing with Homer and one of the belled collars that they now barely noticed when I draped the other one across their necks, each kitten in turn.

It was another week before I was able—very slowly and *veeeeery* cautiously—to fasten around the kittens' necks two collars that had been so greatly loosened, they slipped right off the second a kitten shook their head. Each day I made the collars just a bit tighter with less and less protest from Fanny and Clayton. And—after only two weeks of effort—the collars were on the kittens for good.

FROM THEN ON, AND despite the fact that it was only early May, it was Christmas every day in our home—or, at least, it *sounded* like Christmas every day in our home. A merry, sleigh bell-like jingling rang through our rooms and halls and formed the background accompaniment for just about everything we did. From five-thirty in the morning, when I woke up, until some nineteen hours later, when Laurence went to bed, and then all through the night, the happy, jingle-jangle sound of two intrepid and endlessly active kittens festooned in belled collars pealed out. For the first couple of weeks, until we got accustomed to the sound to not hear it much anymore, it was as if some maddened composer—who'd rigorously confined himself to writing music for a single instrument—had moved in with us. I found myself brushing my teeth in time to the silvery tinkling of the bells, unconsciously punching the keys on my computer to the rhythm of that old "Sleigh Ride" song as I wrote. I'd come upon Laurence in the living room,

reading a newspaper and—clearly without realizing he was doing it—slapping his hand rhythmically on the coffee table, and I
knew that, somewhere in the back of his mind, he was hearing,
Giddy-up! Giddy-up! Giddy-up, let's go... Sometimes I'd awaken
in the dark from dreams of snow and sleds and, in momentary
confusion, wonder why the bedroom air conditioner was running
in the winter, or how the hallway—as I wandered toward the bathroom—could possibly be so warm in the depths of December.

The sound of tinkling bells had once been Homer's very favorite
sound in the world, and it was something he now heard constantly—so constantly that I think it must have been confusing for him
at first. So much ringing in our house! As if all the belled toys in
the world had been trucked in just for him! When the relentless
chiming of bells had finally become overwhelming to the point
that Homer—at long last roused from his grief-inspired languor
to a near-maddened frenzy of playfulness—leapt upon the source
of the ringing, only to find a kitten (and not, say, a toy mouse)
squirming beneath him, he seemed perplexed. *Why do you sound
like a toy?* the startled look on his face telegraphed, before he angrily
slapped at whichever kitten it was who'd "fooled" him into getting
up from his slumbering position on the couch, and all for nothing.

In short order, however, Homer learned that the silvery sound
of a tiny bell ringing was likeliest to mean that Clayton or Fanny,
and not some new toy, was approaching. Which isn't to say that he
entirely gave up the idea that anything with a tinkling bell attached
was a plaything just for him. Although he did come to understand
that the belled collars were *attached* to the kittens, he seemed unwilling to accept the idea that they were *for* the kittens. Apparently
believing that the kittens had somehow commandeered a ringing
toy that was in fact meant for him, he'd do his darnedest to get it
"back"—and Clayton was the most frequent target of his raids.

Fanny wasn't afraid of Homer, exactly—she made, for example, a regular habit of sleeping near him on the couch whenever she was ready to settle in for a nice long nap. But Fanny was a shy little girl, and more respectful by nature than Clayton was. After the first few times Homer had greeted her hesitant overtures toward friendliness with an admonishing paw slap, she'd learned to let Homer himself choose the times and manners in which they might play together—and to give him a wide berth the rest of the time.

Clayton, on the other hand, was as persistent in his pursuit of Homer as Homer had once been in his pursuit of Scarlett, no matter how many times Homer delivered a warning paw slap. *Hey—quit it!* Actually, Clayton was more persistent. He followed Homer absolutely everywhere—if Homer loped down the hallway, then Clayton hippity-hopped after him as fast as his three legs could carry him. If Homer batted a ball of paper across the room, Clayton would eagerly bat it back in Homer's direction—which would only confuse Homer's finely honed sense, perfected by a blind cat over a period of years, as to the exact trajectory a paper ball slapped by him would take. Clayton's interference caused Homer to "lose" his toys more often than not, whereas Clayton couldn't have been more pleased with himself—or more bewildered when Homer would wander off after only one or two back-and-forth volleys. *Look, Homer! I'm playing the same game you are! Hey—where are you going?!!?* If Homer so much as went to use the litter box, Clayton would be waiting impatiently for him just outside. *Whatcha doing in there, Homer? Do you think you'll want to play some more when you're finished?*

No matter how many times Homer slapped or snarled at Clayton, Clayton refused to accept that Homer wasn't as fascinated by him as he was by Homer. Clayton was very far from being the first to wonder how it could be possible to be so obsessed with someone that your entire day revolved around whatever he might be doing at any given moment—and yet, somehow, that someone barely seemed to know or care that you were alive.

As the days went by, however, Homer did begin to show some interest in Clayton—or, rather, in that belled collar that Clayton wore about his neck. Since Homer assumed that the collar was an especially intriguing toy that was his by rights—as all belled toys in our home had always been intended primarily for Homer—he saw no reason why he shouldn't just take it from Clayton. The fact that Clayton was actually *wearing* this particular "toy" was, at most, a minor inconvenience, as far as Homer was concerned.

Accordingly, he would crouch down, poised to spring out at Clayton, whenever he heard the sound of a bell attached to a three-legged kitten approaching, leaping on poor Clayton un-awares, pinning him squealing to the ground, and using his teeth to pry the breakaway collar from around Clayton's neck. Then would begin a dedicated game of Keep Away as a somewhat clumsy Clayton—hampered in any game requiring speed by having only three legs—pursued Homer up and down the hallway; up, over, and around the bed; and across counter tops in a fruitless effort to keep up with his fleet-footed idol and snag his collar—that collar he detested wearing in the first place—back from the vise-like grip of Homer's jaw.

That Clayton positively loathed having to wear that collar was abundantly obvious in the unwonted ingenuity he employed in devising ways to get out of it—an ingenuity that was all the more impressive considering how...perhaps the best word is "lim-ited"...Clayton's understanding was in general.

Clayton was the sweetest little kitten imaginable (so mushy, and sooooooo adorable!), but he was very, *very* far from being the brightest cat I'd ever shared my home with. He was, for example, forever plunging his head into boots and sneakers (Clayton being, for unknown reasons, a passionate connoisseur of human foot odor) and then getting it stuck, so that Laurence or I would have to help pull his head out. He was constantly hurling his toys beneath the couch where he couldn't reach them, and then—due to a particularly roly-poly belly—getting trapped at the halfway point as he tried to wriggle under the couch after them, so that Laurence or I would have to grasp Clayton around his midsection and gently tug until he was freed. He was always falling over sideways while trying to scratch behind his ear, chewing on anything wooden (before I learned to hide all wooden objects) until either he cracked a tooth or ended up with a gumful of splinters, crawling into paper bags and then wailing in alarm because—since his hindquarters were facing the bag's entrance—he couldn't figure out how to get back out of the bag. (Thus giving the lie to the very concept of, *the cat's out of the bag!*) For the entire seven years of his existence and to this day, he has remained firmly convinced that the "falling man" in the *Mad Men* opening credits sequence is actually going to fall right on top of him. (*He's coming right at us! RUN FOR IT!!!*)

But the one thing that Clayton was an absolute expert at was divesting himself of his belled collar—and the only thing he hated more than Homer stealing it from him was actually having to wear it. Despite his apparent difficulty in learning in other areas of his life, with astonishing quickness Clayton groked the breakaway nature of the collar, understanding that a certain amount of pressure applied in the correct spot and for long enough would cause it to break apart and fall free of his neck. Even if I cinched the collar on as tightly as it would go without actually threatening Clayton's breathing, he'd manage to patiently work a paw beneath it and then push against the collar until it broke apart, or somehow wedge it on a corner of the coffee table and tug until he broke free of the collar. Sometimes I noted that, if Fanny's teeth landed on the collar during one of their endless mutual-grooming sessions, he'd pull his whole head backward with a sudden jerk, so that Fanny was left with the collar in her mouth while a triumphant Clayton would scoot away, collar- and fancy-free.

Many was the time when Laurence and I would hear the particularly loud jangle of a belled collar as we watched Clayton tearing up the hallway, and then back down, hippity-hopping at top speed back and forth for no apparent reason other than the demands of kitten logic—and then, the fourth or fifth time he came back into view at the end of the hallway closest to the living room, his approach would be silent—the belled collar lying abandoned on the floor at the far end of the hallway. Clayton seemed happy enough to forget its existence unless Homer happened upon it a few minutes later—gleefully tossing it up and down in his mouth a few times, just to hear it jingle—at which point Clayton, full of righteous indignation, would chase after Homer, squeaking furiously at his big brother and demanding its return.

I spent an inordinate amount of each day reattaching Clayton's collar around his reluctant neck, while he looked up at me with unhappy eyes that eloquently asked, *Geez, mom...do I have to wear it?* But to see Homer up and playing and running around just like his good old self—the way he'd been only a few months ago, before we'd lost Scarlett—made the effort worthwhile. And Homer—who now spent a not-insignificant portion of his own day stalking the sound of ringing bells through our home, a miniature panther in an urban savannah tracking his prey—seemed to be of the same opinion.

The whole point of the belled collars had been to create opportunities for Homer to play with the kittens if and when he wanted to—or to ignore them altogether, if that was his prefer-ence—without having to spend his time dreading that a kitten might be about to sneak up on him or catch him unawares by landing atop him with a wild leap while he was doing something else.

What I hadn't anticipated was that the bells themselves would be what brought Homer back to us.

In our moments of greatest sorrow, we all have an idea of the things that might lift our spirits, if only a little—an old movie, perhaps, or a spontaneous shopping expedition, or some favorite childhood food that only your grandmother knew how to make just the way you liked it. (My own grandmother was, to my knowl-edge, the only living human being who knew just the right amount of sugar to add to a bowlful of chopped banana and sour cream to make it absolute perfection.) The idea of "comfort food" can be extended to include any number of sights, tastes, and smells. And, for a blind cat, "comfort food" could, of course, be a sound as well. Homer's favorite stuffed worm—the beloved, if inanimate, best friend of his earliest kitten-hood—had had a little silver bell attached to its tail. So had all of the toys Homer had loved when he was young. And the sound of a bell ringing in another room had always meant, to Homer, that one of his much-loved older sis-ters was playing with something—that maybe if he ran in quickly enough, and tried enthusiastically enough, *this* time would be the time when one or the other of them would finally include him in their games.

The only true misfortune in Homer's life wasn't his blindness, which at any rate never struck him as being nearly as important as it seemed to those around him. It was that a cat as filled with love as Homer was had, through a quirk of fate, wound up with two older sisters who probably did love him—grudgingly, in their own way—but who never felt the need to demonstrate that love in any of the tactile ways (grooming, cuddling, affectionate tail brushes in passing) that would have meant the world to a blind cat for whom touch, in the absence of sight, took on even greater significance.

And now, at the very end of his life, Homer found himself veritably surrounded by love—by two little kittens who were wildly, goofily, insanely in love with him. Kittens who—if only given the chance, if Homer would just let them get close enough—would never get tired of showing him just how much they adored him. The sound of bells ringing in our home no longer just represented an interesting toy, or cats playing at a distance who might or might not let Homer play with them for a moment or two. A bell ringing now meant the approach of a kitten willing to lick Homer's muzzle, to curl up for warmth against his belly on the couch, to play any game Homer might feel like playing for however long Homer felt like playing it, on the sole condition that he would let them join in.

As for me, among my own favorite sights and sounds had always been those of Homer racing around our home, busy at his "job" of playing and running and just generally being a happy cat. Whenever I heard the sound of a belled kitten whooshing by, I knew that, coming right after it, would be the sound of Homer—high-spirited and himself once again—chasing after. I would reflect sometimes on the miracle of it—that Homer, so late in life, would finally find so much of the love he must have thought he'd lost with Scarlett not only returned to him, but returned to him tenfold. If Clayton and Fanny have grown up a little spoiled—perhaps just a *tiny* bit overindulged and doted upon—it's only because, to this day, I can't love them or thank them enough for ensuring that my last memories of Homer are as filled with joy and laughter as my earliest ones are.

I'd thought at first that constantly hearing ringing bells in our home—from morning until night, in the background of every single thing Laurence and I did or said—might drive me a little crazy. Eventually, though, it wasn't just that I got used to it. The sound of bells ringing meant that my little feline family was happy and, once again, complete. Very often, as I wrote or showered or did a spot of housecleaning, I'd catch myself, without realizing it, singing under my breath: *Just hear those sleigh bells jingling, ring-ting-tingling too...*

WE MOVED TO A new home recently, and in the process of packing up our old place I came across any number of things I'd forgotten about that had found their way, over the years, to the bottoms of drawers and untouched closet corners —newspaper clippings containing reviews of my very first book, published way back in 2007; photos of a much-younger me with old friends, taken on Miami Beach's Lincoln Road in bars and restaurants that no longer existed; a diary I'd kept when I was in the third grade, given to me by my grandmother as a Hanukkah gift.

And, buried way back on a top closet shelf, in a small wooden box containing a clipping of Homer's fur and a little plaster imprint of his paw, I found the small pink and blue collars I'd bought for Fanny and Clayton all those years ago. Clayton's blue collar bore the battle scars inflicted by his claws and Homer's teeth, but otherwise they were still in perfect condition—and still jingled out merrily enough when I gave them a shake.

I was unprepared for the flood of memories that hit me—memories of two intrepid kittens, now middle-aged cats, gamboling through the hallways of our old home. Of Homer, who'd been near-catatonic with grief for so many months, chasing playfully after them. Of how welcome the sounds of life and love had been in our apartment after weeks and weeks of sad, relentless silence. And of how quiet it had seemed once again, after Homer went to sleep for the last time, and we'd finally taken belled collars off the kittens for good.

Fanny and Clayton, drawn by the sound of bells, came upstairs to see what I was up to and found me sitting on the closet floor with the belled collars in my hand. I wondered if they remembered these collars, if hearing them brought back any memories of their youth and of Homer. If Homer could somehow be reconstituted and were to materialize now, here, in front of us, would they recognize him? Would they greet him with the same delight that I would greet the old friends in the pictures I'd found, if we ran into each other again? (*It's so great to see you! How many years has it been?!*) Or would Clayton and Fanny look at him blankly, having lost all trace of even the memory of the big brother they'd idolized once upon a time—when they were so tiny that even a small cat like Homer had towered over their lives and imaginations like a colossus.

Fanny gave the collars a cursory sniff and then, bored, wandered off. But Clayton very carefully grasped the battered blue collar in his teeth. Tugging gently, he drew it from my hand and then scurried off with it, the jingling sound of a little silver bell trailing after him through the hallway and down the stairs.

I let him take it, telling myself that I'd find it again before moving day. And I did look for it later. I checked under beds and tables and the sofa, and even behind the refrigerator. I checked high shelves and low corners. *Where could it be?* I asked Laurence in frustration. *Where could he possibly have hidden it?*

Maybe Clayton buried it in the couch we ended up getting rid of before we moved. Maybe he dropped it into one of the innumerable bags of trash and discarded things we threw away before the moving van came. Maybe he lodged it, unnoticed, beneath an old floorboard or some loosened corner of the carpeting.

Maybe it's simply enough to know that not all mysteries in this life have answers.

In any case, moving day came and went, but I never saw the little blue, belled collar again.

CAT BOOKS FOR CAT LOVERS!

Be sure to check out more of *New York Times* bestselling author Gwen Cooper's celebrated books for cat lovers—including tales of her real-life feline family and the world-famous Homer the Blind Wonder Cat!

Get a FREE copy of the book
Homer Returns:
More True Tales of a Blind Wonder Cat & His Fur Family
Visit www.gwencooper.com

CHECK OUT THE
HOMER'S ODYSSEY SCRAPBOOK!

100+ OVERSIZED, full-color pages!

---❄---

Hundreds of never-before-seen photos of Homer from Gwen's own family photo albums!

---❄---

Pages from Gwen's first draft of *Homer's Odyssey* with her editor's handwritten notes!

---❄---

New writing and stories!

---❄---

Much, much more!

Acknowledgments

Heartfelt thanks and profound gratitude to the following people (and cats!), without whom I could never have completed this book.

Special thanks to Patti, Nikolaka & Koa!

- » Diane Aba
- » Alyson Amsterdam (and Louie & Biggie)
- » Margaret Auld-Louie (and Julius & Simba)
- » Jamery Sue Barry (and Colby, Sully, Misty & Georgie)
- » Charles Brackney (and Shane, Chloe & Abby)
- » Dorothy Brown (and Patrick, Camel & Sugar Maple)
- » Jane Broyles
- » Julie Burns
- » Lisa Calarese (and Riley, Mordecai & Rigby)
- » Deborah Foresman (and Tinkerbell)
- » Paul Froiland (and Louie & Fitzy)
- » Meg Galipault (and Scout, Waffles, Sisu, Dru & Huckleberry)
- » Lee-Ann Gilliam
- » Tracy Ginnane
- » Sara Goodman (and Dennis)

- » Wanda Goodwin (and Lewie Stewart)
- » Jill Graves
- » Susan Haenicke (and Bessie & Hamilton)
- » Marianne Harding (and Charles Carlos Ambrose Harding)
- » J. Eric Hoehn
- » Susan Anne Kadlec
- » Julie Kennedy
- » Connie Keith-Kerns (and Zoey, Ari Kai & Mrf)
- » Julie Kennedy
- » Calvin & Eileen Keyser (and Ashes, Ninja & Snickers)
- » Beth Kirby
- » Ken Kistner
- » Ronald Koltnow (and Speedy)
- » Catherine Larklund
- » Louisa Lee
- » Carole Loftin (and Sadie, Biscuit & Brazil)
- » Julie Lowe (and Gracie, Cougar, Java, Raven, Meeko, & Bella)
- » Dolores Manzino (and Antigone "Tiggy")
- » Neta Mercer (and Pouncer, Felix & Snacks)
- » TJ Murphy (and Shelly, Max, Gio & Anna)
- » David Nagreski (and Chassis)
- » Matthew O'Leary (and Hank)
- » Melanie Paradise (and Idia)
- » Teresa Pesce (and TabbyCat)
- » Stephanie Peters (and Max)
- » D.H. Powell IV (and Bobby & Willow)
- » Vanessa Ramirez
- » Stephanie Reicen (and Oliver, Mickey & Helen)
- » Kathryn Rigsby
- » Felicia Roe (and Eurydice & Cassiopeia)

» Janice Rogenski (and Buster, Misty & Alyssa)
» Andrea Sachs (and Abby & Jimmy)
» Kathy Schlichthernlein (and Scrappy & the Gang)
» Zoe Shinno (and Midnite)
» Christine Sorenson
» Emily Stafford (and Randy & Pepper)
» Anne Teghtmeyer
» Lenai Waite (and Martin)
» Allison Walls (and Podo, Rue & Dom)
» Lola Whitehead
» Katie Williams
» Michele Zarichny

About the Author

GWEN COOPER IS THE *New York Times* bestselling author of the memoirs *Homer's Odyssey: A Fearless Feline Tale, or How I Learned About Love and Life with a Blind Wonder Cat*; *Homer: The Ninth Life of a Blind Wonder Cat*; and *My Life in a Cat House: True Tales of Love, Laughter, and Living with Five Felines*, as well as the novel *Love Saves the Day*, narrated from a rescue cat's point of view. Her work has been published in more than two-dozen languages. She is a frequent speaker at shelter fundraisers and donates 10% of her royalties from *Homer's Odyssey* to organizations that serve abused, abandoned, and disabled animals.

Gwen lives in New Jersey with her husband, Laurence. She also lives with her two perfect cats—Clayton "the Tripod" and his litter-mate, Fanny—who aren't impressed with any of it.

Get a FREE copy of an all-new book about Homer and the gang!
Visit www.gwencooper.com

Printed in Great Britain
by Amazon

39069328R00149